Career
Ahead

The Complete Career Handbook

Published by Raleo Publishing Ltd

Set in Enigma 9/11pt

Design by Price Watkins
Printed by Micropress Printers Ltd, Suffolk

A catalogue record for Career Ahead – The Complete Career
Handbook is available from the British Library

ISBN 978-0-9561118-0-7

Editor: Rowan Davies

Career
Ahead

The Complete Career Handbook

JENNY UNGLESS

 **RALEO PUBLISHING**

To Goose

Acknowledgments

First and foremost, thanks to my brilliant publisher Keith, for believing in this project, and in me.

Thanks also to the terrific team at Monster, especially Michelle and Danny, and at Weber Shandwick (Tali, Sneha, Laura and Charlie) – many thanks for all the media opportunities you've given me, and for your support with the book.

And, of course, a huge thank you to all my clients, past and present. It's been a privilege to work with each of you.

Finally, a special thank you to my late friend the Rt Hon Eric Forth MP, who taught me so much about values and priorities.

Contents

Introduction

- Does the thought of Monday morning ruin the weekend for you?
- Are you bored, frustrated and fed up with your work?
- Is the promotion you want eluding you?
- Are you clueless about what to do with your life?
- Do you have an idea of what you'd love to do for a living but no clear plan for achieving it?
- Are you sick of earning money for someone else and desperate to do your own thing?

How much do you love what you do for a living? An amazing number of people (some surveys say as many as 75 per cent of us!) say that they don't enjoy their work. If you're one of them, then this book is for you. You owe it to yourself to do work that you love. This book will show you how.

Perhaps you're completely confused about what you want to do with your life and where your career is going. You might feel that you've taken the wrong career path but have no idea what job you'd really like. Maybe you've got to the point where you resent the fact that work is getting in the way of your life. Or you might just be feeling a bit disillusioned or generally unexcited about your job.

If none of these situations applies, put this back for someone who needs it more and browse something else! If any of it sounds familiar, however, read on.

How this book can help

When I say that this book is a complete career handbook, that's exactly what I mean. It covers every aspect of career planning, from how to work out what you want to do in the first place, through to how to land the job you want and how to make an impact when you get there. You'll also find out about other ways of working, including the option of setting up your own business. And you'll learn how to tackle the most common problems that people face at work, such as procrastination and managing your time.

The book is divided into 4 parts. **Part 1** is for you if you have no idea what you want to do with your life. It explains the factors you really need to think about to help you make career decisions that suit you, and gives you tools and exercises to make that thinking process easier.

Part 2 guides you through the whole process of getting the job you want. It shows you how to put together a stunning CV, gives you a wide range of strategies and tactics for searching out opportunities and securing interviews, and advises how to negotiate the right benefits package.

Part 3 will help you to make a big impression in your new role, or to make improvements in your current one. It shows you how to make an early impact, and explains the attitudes and actions that will help you build your reputation and put you on the fast-track to promotion.

Part 4 is for those of you thinking about setting up your own business. It shows you how to come up with a business idea, and how to make it happen.

So, whatever your professional situation, there's something here for you. And the support doesn't stop there: by logging on to our website www.citylifecoaching.com you can email our careers coaches with your questions.

You'll spend the best part of 100,000 hours of your life at work, which is a pretty long time if you don't enjoy what you do. This book will show you how to turn your career around so that Monday mornings are something to look forward to, not to dread. Yes, it can be done!

Part 1
Finding Your Niche

Chapter 1

The Changing World of Work?

There is a lot of received wisdom and anecdotal evidence about how the world of work is changing. For example, there's a widespread perception that, at the beginning of the 21st century, work is more flexible, more short-term and less secure than it has ever been before. How much of this is reality, though, and how much simply perception? And what do the real trends in the way we work mean for how we plan and manage our careers?

Let's look at the facts.

FACT 1: Society is ageing.

Life expectancy is increasing, and the ratio of people at work to people in retirement is falling. That means fewer people of working age to support those who have retired, and that in turn is likely to mean a bigger drain on our incomes as the Government uses tax, among other things, to square the funding circle. This, to put it simply, means less money in your pay packet. And because current life-expectancy rates suggest that you're likely to live until well into your eighties, you're going to have to work longer before you can afford to retire. If you're now in your twenties or thirties, you could be looking at working into your seventies, or beyond.

FACT 2: The emotional and legal contract between employers and employees is changing.

The world is speeding up, and companies who want to stay ahead of the increasingly global competition have to be fast, flexible and dynamic. They have to have employees with today's and tomorrow's skills, not yesterday's. 'Jobs for life' are becoming rarer – or, at least, we think they are; our feelings of job insecurity have soared over the last decade. In a world of ever-tighter profit margins, companies are increasingly outsourcing aspects of their work to keep overheads down. And, of course, if members of staff aren't permanent, then there's not much incentive for an employer to invest in their career management and development. Even where roles are still permanent (and the prediction is that most of us *will* still be in permanent roles by 2020), personnel and career management services are often the first victims of a cost-cutting exercise. Many companies know that they should think about staff development, succession planning and so on, but in practice they can find it difficult to prioritise these things.

FACT 3: Technology has dramatically altered the relationship between our work and our personal lives.

The internet has greatly increased the amount of information that we have available to us, and therefore have to deal with. Mobile phones, email and the dreaded Blackberry have made us contactable around the clock, and blurred the boundaries between work and home. Of course, there's a positive side to these developments – it can make it easier to work flexibly, for example – but the effect for most professionals is that the pace of work has intensified, and we're working longer hours. A recent survey by the employment law firm Peninsula found that, over the last last ten years, the average working week has increased by a full day.

FACT 4: Over the past decade, we have become much less happy at work.

Research found a significant reduction in job satisfaction rates during the 1990s. I suspect that this is a natural consequence of Fact 3: we are working longer hours and it's much harder than it used to be to get away from the office completely. It might also be linked to Fact 5.

FACT 5: We are becoming more aspirational.

Sociologists have charted a growing shift away from materialism towards self-expression and fulfilment. The growth of the health, wellbeing and self-help sectors reflects this, but it applies to the world of work as well. A recent survey of 25-year-olds by the website eBay showed that a desire for 'personal fulfilment' was the main career motivator for 74 per cent of respondents. Another study showed that nearly nine out of ten young people are seeking careers that will 'add purpose to their lives'. That said, research has shown that those in their twenties and thirties are still overwhelmingly conservative, moderate and conformist (their main ambitions involve housing, careers, marriage and children), but their expectations are higher and they're less prepared to settle for anything that is less than perfect.

FACT 6: We're more ready to experiment.

In 1975, within three years of entering employment young people under 25 would have expected to be in their second job; in the 1990s, they would have expected to be in their fourth. This might be linked to Fact 5, or it might be that, in an increasingly consumer-led society, we are simply used to having more choice. The internet has also encouraged many young professionals to adopt an experimental 'job-shopping' approach; there are so many opportunities advertised on the net, and it's quick and easy to apply online. Together, Facts 5 and 6 go a long way towards explaining the appearance of YEPPIEs: young experimenting perfection-seekers. (And no, I did not come up with that one.)

So, what are the implications of these facts for your career?

1   You're probably going to have to work into your seventies before you can afford to retire. That's at least 100,000 hours of work, so you owe it to yourself to do something you enjoy.
2   You can't depend on your employers to look after your career; they will have too much on their own plates. You are the only person you should trust with this responsibility.
3   The boundary between work and personal life is becoming more and more blurred; it's going to be up to you to sort out your work–life balance.
4   More and more of us want a greater sense of fulfilment from our work, but only you can identify exactly what this means for you.
5   We have access to more information and more choices than ever before. There's really no excuse for not finding a career that you enjoy.

Ready to do that? Read on...

Chapter 2

Your Values

Before we get down to the detail of what you need to think about to help you plan your career path, I want you to spend some time looking at your life as a whole. Why? Because *your work is not your life*. As a career coach, I believe that we owe it to ourselves to do work that we enjoy: work that has some meaning to us and gives us a sense of purpose. But it shouldn't be the only important thing in our lives. Most of our significant memories and experiences come from outside work; your friends and family, rather than your colleagues, are the ones who really find you indispensable. As the old saying goes, no one lies on their deathbed wishing they'd spent more time in the office.

Having said that, your work should add to, not detract from, your enjoyment of the rest of your life. This isn't just about the hours you work (although of course that is relevant); it's about having a job from which you come home excited and energised, not emotionally and physically drained. It's about doing something that genuinely interests you, using your natural skills and talents. It's about being in a professional environment that allows you to be 'you'.

However, to be brutally honest, it's pretty hard to find a job that you love 100 per cent. Even those of us who feel that we have found our niche find that there are elements of our work that we don't enjoy. I hate administration work, for example, but it takes up a fairly small amount of my time, so I tolerate it. If I got really fed up, I'd contract it out. The point is that most of us have lots of scope to increase our level of job satisfaction.

And that's what I'm going to help you to do, starting by looking at your values and what you actually want to get from your work.

Your decision about what career is right for you has to be put in the context of the kind of life you want to have. As I've said, your career is one element of your life, but it shouldn't be your whole life. What your work should do is facilitate, support and complement your lifestyle. For that to happen, you need to be clear about the life and lifestyle that you want. This will give you the context and framework for your career planning.

The fundamental starting point is working out what is important to you: your *values*. There are two kinds of values: *intrinsic* or internal (essentially to do with how you relate to the world and other people –honesty, independence, connection); and *extrinsic* (essentially to do with external factors such as money, health and your environment). Both types are important. Focusing on your values will help you to:

1   make lifestyle choices that are right for you;
2   get the right balance between life and work; and

3   make good career and work choices.

Focus on what your values are by going through the exercises below. Don't panic if this feels a bit daunting: many people find this to be the hardest part of the whole career-planning process, but it's also the most important. Give yourself plenty of time to complete the exercises. Don't worry if you can't answer all the questions the first time around; it's a good idea to have an initial go, then leave them aside for a few days and come back to them.

A word of advice: be as honest as you can. Don't list values that you think you *ought* to have: list the ones that you *do* have. So, if money is important to you, write it down (although see my comments on money below!). If fame and recognition are important, then ditto. There are no 'right' or 'wrong' answers; what you are doing is trying to identify and articulate what really motivates you. You're trying to pin down what's really important to you and what *you* really want. If you've spent your time so far trying to live up to other people's expectations, it will take time to change your perspective. It's crucial that you are totally honest in this exercise because, if you aren't, you will end up making lifestyle and career choices based on someone else's values, and you'll be miserable.

Now, a word about money. Lots of people identify money as a value, but it's useful to remember that the real value of money is what it allows you to do: for example, to have more freedom, to travel, to spend less time working, to buy the things that give you pleasure. So if money is one of the values you choose, try to think about what it actually is that you want your money to *buy*. This is particularly important in terms of your career choices; for example, if the reason you want more money is so that you can travel more, then there's little point in taking a job that pays really well but requires you to work long hours and take fewer holidays.

Values exercise
Have a look at the matrix below and circle all of the values that are important to you. Add any others that occur to you and are missing. Now narrow it down to the ten that you feel are *really* important. Finally, whittle your list down to the four words that best represent the person you are. These are your essential values, the things that you should be seeking to base your lifestyle and career choices on. (No one's saying that the average person has only four values, by the way! But being forced to narrow down your choices helps you to focus on your real priorities.)

Abundance	Connection	Creativity	Honesty
Acceptance	Joy	Adventure	Passion
Influence	Security	Courage	Freedom
Family	Achievement	Integrity	Consistency

Fun	Education	Compassion	Health
Capability	Love	Relationships	Control
Excellence	Delight	Independence	Improvement
Originality	Community	Money	Peace
Responsibility	Spontaneity	Perception	Contentment
Unity	Competition	Strength	Trust
Challenge	Service	Support	Quality
Power	Excitement	Friendship	Respect
Time	Success	Privacy	Self-esteem
Standards	Choice	Distinction	Justice
Routine	Prestige	Morality	Recognition
Serenity	Risk	Faith	Balance

For each of the core values that you have identified, try to define exactly what it means to you. For example, if you've chosen 'fun', what precisely do you mean by that? What's *your* definition of fun? Be as specific as you can.

Values and lifestyle choices
Now use your values to help you build up a clearer picture of how you'd like your life and lifestyle to be. First of all, think about your current situation: what's working well, and which areas of your life are you less happy with? For each of the categories in the table below, take a few minutes to write a description of this aspect of your life as it currently stands. The questions listed beside each category will help you with this. How would you rate each category on a scale of one to ten, where one is 'this sucks' and ten is 'brilliant'?

Category	Questions to ask yourself
Physical environment	Do I love the country/city/town/community that I live in? Do I feel at home here? Do I have enough space for me? Do I have too many possessions, or too few? What would I love to own that I currently don't?
Health	How happy am I with my fitness and appearance? Do I make enough time to exercise and do I enjoy the exercise that I do? Do I eat well?
Finances	Am I content with my level of income? Am I worried about debt? Do I have time to spend the money I earn in ways that bring me pleasure? Have I got a good financial management plan in place or do I worry that I often fritter money away? Am I concerned about my financial future?
Career	Do I enjoy getting up in the morning to go to work? Do I feel that I have found my niche, or am I usually disengaged from work? How much time do I spend clock-watching at work, or daydreaming

	about doing something completely different? Am I paid enough for what I do?
Friends/family	Am I happy that I have enough time to spend with friends and family? Do those relationships enhance my life, or do I feel drained by the people around me? Who would I like to see more/less of?
Partner/relationship	How close do I feel to my partner? How much of our time together is 'quality' time? If I'm single, am I happy with that situation?
Fun/recreation	How much time do I spend every week on my favourite hobbies and activities? How does this compare with the amount of time I spend on things I don't enjoy? Do I feel that life is fun or dreary? How stressed am I?

For the areas in which your scores are quite low, think carefully about the extent to which your true values are reflected in your current situation. For example, if time and freedom are important to you, but you seldom get the chance to spend quality time by yourself because you're so busy with work or bogged down with clutter at home, you're going to score badly because the reality is so out of synch with what actually matters to you.

The question you need to ask yourself in relation to each category is: *What changes do I need to make so that I am living in accordance with my values?* Asking this question for each category in turn will help you to pin down exactly where you need to make changes. It's much easier than asking yourself vague questions about what you want your 'perfect life' to look like.

Think about the overall balance of these categories. Which ones are the most important to you? Which categories do you need to focus on to make the biggest change in your overall happiness?

This is a book about your career, so I'm guessing that many of you will have given that category quite a low score (if not, why are you reading this?). But before we move on to focus on work issues, take a moment to consider other categories in which your score is not too high. To what extent is that linked to the fact that you are unhappy in your work? For example, if your relationship with your partner is not as good as you'd like, how much of that is down to the fact that you work such long hours that you never see them, or when you get home from work you're so fed up that you take your bad mood out on them? Your career has a direct knock-on effect on every other category in the list above: your finances, your friendships, your health and your leisure time. That's why it makes so much sense to get it right. However, if you have identified other areas in which you need to make changes, this is the time to acknowledge that.

Using your values to set your goals

You've given some thought to what's really important to you, and the changes you'd need to make in your life so that you are living in accordance with your values. Now use that information to set yourself some goals. What do you want to achieve in each area of your life over the next six months? The next year? The next three years? Make your goals as tangible as possible. You might have come across the idea of setting SMART goals: goals that are specific, measurable, achievable, realistic and timed. In other words, what exactly do you want to achieve, and by when? How will you know when you've achieved it? What will be the benefit to you of achieving it? How will your life be different?

Spend some time on this exercise. The more precise you can be about what your goals are, the more chance you have of achieving them. Do write them down: research demonstrates that people who write down their goals are much more likely to achieve them. Why? I'm not sure! Maybe because they're more focused, or because writing out your goals forces you to articulate them more precisely, or because written-down goals act as a constant reminder of where you're trying to get to (assuming you look at them from time to time, that is!). Whatever the reason, the evidence is that it works, so do it. Some of your goals might be a little bit fuzzy at this stage, especially your career ones (which is why you're reading this book, after all). But even if you don't know exactly what you want to do with your career, you know that you want to make changes. Ask yourself when you want these changes to occur, and write that down. As you work through this book, you'll find your specific career goals getting clearer and clearer.

Values and career choices

On that note, let's turn the spotlight back on to your career. Again, it should come as no surprise to you that the starting point for making good career choices is your list of values. Your values tell you what makes you tick. They describe what you care about, what you enjoy, and which kinds of working cultures and environments will suit you. If you want to have a job that you love, you need to base your choices on your fundamental values. It's as simple as that.

You should use your core values to help you identify things that are non-negotiable in terms of your career. This exercise is really useful not only in helping you to assess the suitability of different career options, but also in helping you to differentiate between potential employers, even within the same industry. Companies differ widely in terms of culture, objectives and how they treat their employees. Finding a company or organisation whose values match your own is critical to your job satisfaction; if your work environment doesn't value the same things that you do, you're going to find it very difficult to stay motivated and engaged.

The trick is to take your chosen values and turn them into a set of benchmark questions. For each of the values and priorities that you have identified, work out the question that you need to ask of any particular employer or role. Look at the example below to help you get started.

Value	Question(s) I need to answer
Independence	What is the management structure? Where do I fit into it? What are my reporting lines and how closely will I be managed on a day-to-day basis? What scope will I have for introducing my own ideas and ways of doing things?
Prestige	How highly regarded is the industry/company? How proud would I be to say I worked in this industry/company? How are employees of this company regarded within the industry? How does the company reward them?
Fun	How vibrant is the industry/company? Does it take itself too seriously? Does it promote a good work–life balance among employees? How sociable is it?

Your questions will probably be a mixture of practical ones related to your extrinsic values, and slightly less tangible ones relating to your intrinsic values. The practical, extrinsic questions will be quite easy to answer or research (How long would my commute be?). The questions relating to your intrinsic values will probably revolve around how well your values are likely to fit with those of your prospective employer (How much autonomy/recognition would I get? How ethical is the company?). We'll deal with how to find out the *answers* to these questions when we talk about job searching and interviews (see Part 2), but for now just be aware that the clearer you can be about what you really need from your working environment, the easier it will be for you to achieve it.

If you've been working through the exercises (and, if you haven't, I do suggest you go back and do them before moving on to the next chapter), you should now have a much clearer picture of what is and isn't working in your life as a whole, and the areas in which you need to make changes.

You will also have a list of key criteria to help you make career choices. We'll come back to these in Chapter 5 when we look at pulling together all the information you're amassing about yourself, but now we're going to move on and consider some other key factors in helping you think about work: your **skills**, your **strengths** and your **style**.

Chapter 3

Your Skills, Strengths and Style

As we saw in Chapter 2, focusing on your values allows to you put in place the foundations of a satisfying career. To continue the analogy, the two main building blocks of successful career planning are your **skills** and your **interests**. This chapter is about your skills, and Chapter 4 will deal with your interests.

Your skills

The starting point in identifying the sort of role that will suit you is a **skills audit**. A word of warning here: don't be tempted to rush this section on the basis that you've done a skills analysis before, or that you already know what your skills are. Most people undersell themselves hugely because they have too limited a picture of their skill-set. Many tend to focus on their current job when they try to list their skills but, if you're in a job you don't enjoy, the chances are that you're not actually using some or all of your core skills. We're going to get you to think about your skills in a range of different ways, so that you build up as comprehensive a picture as possible.

Let's start with the basics. Go through the list below and pick out the skills that you have. Divide them into three categories: skills with **people** (for example, coaching); skills with **information** (for example, analysing); and skills with **things** (for example, building).

Achieving	Acting	Adapting	Addressing	Administering
Advising	Analysing	Anticipating	Arbitrating	Arranging
Ascertaining	Assembling	Assessing	Attaining	Auditing
Budgeting	Building	Calculating	Caring	Checking
Classifying	Coaching	Collecting	Communicating	Compiling
Completing	Composing	Computing	Conceptualising	Conducting
Conserving	Consolidating	Constructing	Controlling	Coordinating
Coping	Counselling	Creating	Decision-making	Delegating
Delivering	Designing	Detailing	Detecting	Determining
Developing	Diagnosing	Directing	Discovering	Dramatising
Editing	Eliminating	Empathising	Enforcing	Establishing
Estimating	Evaluating	Examining	Experimenting	Explaining
Fixing	Following	Formulating	Guiding	Handling
Identifying	Imagining	Implementing	Improving	Improvising

Increasing	Influencing	Informing	Initiating	Innovating
Inspecting	Inspiring	Installing	Instituting	Instructing
Integrating	Interpreting	Interviewing	Intuiting	Inventing
Investigating	Judging	Leading	Learning	Listening
Maintaining	Making	Managing	Manipulating	Mediating
Meeting	Memorising	Mentoring	Modelling	Monitoring
Motivating	Navigating	Negotiating	Observing	Obtaining
Offering	Operating	Ordering	Organising	Originating
Overseeing	Perceiving	Persuading	Planning	Predicting
Preparing	Prescribing	Presenting	Prioritising	Problem-solving
Processing	Producing	Programming	Projecting	Promoting
Protecting	Providing	Publicising	Purchasing	Questioning
Reasoning	Recommending	Recruiting	Relating	Remembering
Reporting	Representing	Researching	Resolving	Reviewing
Risk-taking	Scheduling	Selecting	Selling	Sensing
Solving	Sorting	Speaking	Studying	Summarising
Supervising	Surveying	Taking instructions	Taking responsibility	Talking
Teaching	Team-building	Training	Troubleshooting	Understanding

Now, here's the most important part of the exercise: take your list of skills and highlight the ones that you *most enjoy using*. In other words, which tasks and activities really give you a buzz? Which tasks are you carrying out and which skills are you using when you are so engrossed that you don't notice time passing?

Be as specific as you can. So, for example, don't just say that you like 'communicating'. Flesh out the detail: do you like to communicate orally or in writing? If it's orally, do you like to make formal presentations to big groups, or do you prefer to talk less formally to a smaller group, or one-on-one? What sorts of things do you like communicating? For example, do you enjoy passing on factual information from a position of expertise, or do you prefer to facilitate a brainstorming session? Think through the detail of how you like to use each skill. Come up with specific examples of times when you have been really happy or engaged with your work. Which skills were you using? What exactly did you achieve and how?

Your favourite skills are the ones you should be focusing on because they are the ones that will bring you the most satisfaction. We all have things that we are perfectly capable of doing, but that don't bring us much pleasure (my tax return for example). Being good at something isn't enough of a reason to spend lots of time doing it. Of course, as we've said before, most jobs will have some elements that you don't really enjoy, but about three-quarters of your time at work should be spent using the skills that you really love to use. Anything less and you're selling yourself short.

When you're putting together your list of favourite skills, don't focus only on skills that you use in your current job, or have used in previous jobs. Think about activities that you enjoy outside work as well, and the skills you're using when you engage in them. In particular, think about the role you tend to play when you are with groups of friends: do you always ends up doing the organising, or do you make sure no one is left out, or do you act as mediator if other friends have had an argument? Think about what your friends and family instinctively turn to you for. What do people compliment you on? What do you find easy that other people find hard? Again, concentrate on the things that you enjoy: if you love organising everyone's social life then add that to your list, but don't include it if it's something that you often end up doing but resenting.

Finally, look at all the favourite skills you have identified and see whether you can find some themes. Are most of your skills people-orientated, for example? Are there two or more skills that could be grouped under one word or heading? For example, you might have listed mentoring, coaching and inspiring. Is there one category of skill that outshines the others? On the other hand, perhaps you have listed a wide range of skills that do not seem to be related. That might point to the fact that you are suited more to a generalist than a specialist role.

Your strengths

In Chapter 5 we'll look at how to use your skills analysis to identify roles to suit you, but first let's take some time to think about your **strengths**. The distinction between strengths and skills is sometimes a little fuzzy, but in general I define skills as things that you have learned to do (whether taught by yourself or others), while strengths are natural characteristics (anything from generosity to a sense of humour to an attitude of curiosity about the world). The eminent psychologist Martin Seligman has identified 24 different strengths, and if you go to his website at www.authentichappiness.org, you can take his strengths test for free. I've suggested that you should be looking to spend three-quarters of your time at work using the skills that you most enjoy. Similarly, Seligman suggests that we can make our work much more satisfying by finding opportunities to use our key (or 'signature') strengths. Moreover, thinking about your strengths is incredibly useful not only in helping you to identify roles that will suit you, but also in helping you to describe yourself to a prospective employer; it's important to be able to talk about the kind of person that you are, as well as your work experience and achievements.

Another way to focus on your strengths is to think back to situations in which you did something well. Think about successes that you have had. What was it about your attitude or behaviour that contributed to or caused the success? Come up with as many examples as you can of things you have done well, and try to identify exactly what it was that led to the successful outcome. Look for recurring patterns of behaviour; these are your strengths, and they are approaches and attributes that you should be looking to incorporate into any work that you do.

A further quick word about strengths and weaknesses. You may well have come across the approach of analysing your (or your organisation's) strengths and weaknesses, the idea being that you build on your strengths and work to overcome your weaknesses. In a business environment, it's a sensible approach, but it's not one that I buy into when it comes to career planning. To be blunt, I take the view that you should focus almost exclusively on your strengths. If you have an area of weakness, what that means is that there are types of tasks or work situations that you don't enjoy, in which you don't perform well and that don't give you a sense of achievement or satisfaction. The best thing to do is to recognise what these tasks and situations are and make sure that you avoid them as far as possible. Too many of us operate in work environments that don't suit us, so that we end up role-playing. While it's good to push yourself to operate outside your comfort zone from time to time (because it helps you to develop), having to do this too often actually has a negative effect on your confidence. It also means that you have to devote a lot of emotional energy to looking as though you can do the job, which detracts from your ability to perform well. So, you need to be aware of the sorts of things you don't like doing and make sure that your job involves as few of them as possible.

Of course, as I've already said, it's difficult to find a role in which you love absolutely every aspect of what you do, but remember that every minute that you spend on tasks you don't enjoy and that grind you down is a minute wasted. People who have great careers are people who spend a disproportionate amount of time doing the things they love and have a natural talent for.

Your style

Finally, think about your **style**: your personality traits and characteristics. How do you naturally tend to approach situations and tasks? For example, are you someone who is quick to reach judgements and make choices, or do you tend to work through options in a methodical way before reaching a decision? Do you like to know your subject thoroughly before you engage with a colleague or customer, or are you the kind of person who gets a buzz from having to 'wing it' occasionally? Do you enjoy the opportunity to be creative and think laterally, or do you work better in an environment that is process-oriented, with clear rules and operating procedures? There's really no 'right' or 'wrong' answer on any of this; the secret is to analyse the way that you tend to handle situations.

You should be looking to ensure that your professional style is as close as possible to your natural personal style. In other words, you need to be in a role or work environment that not only allows you to be yourself, but in which your personal style and approach is in fact the secret of your success. You don't want to be in a role that doesn't make you feel like 'you'.

Use the list of traits below to help you identify the aspects of your character that sum up your style.

Accurate	Discreet	Practical
Achievement-orientated	Dynamic	Professional
Adaptable	Economical	Protective
Adept	Effective	Punctual
Adventurous	Energetic	Quick
Alert	Enthusiastic	Rational
Appreciative	Experienced	Realistic
Assertive	Expert	Reliable
Astute	Firm	Resourceful
Authoritative	Flexible	Responsible
Calm	Impulsive	Responsive
Cautious	Independent	Self-motivated
Charismatic	Innovative	Self-reliant
Competent	Knowledgeable	Sensitive
Consistent	Loyal	Sophisticated
Cooperative	Methodical	Strong
Courageous	Objective	Supportive
Creative	Open-minded	Tactful
Decisive	Outgoing	Thorough
Deliberate	Patient	Unique
Dependable	Perceptive	Unusual
Diligent	Persistent	Versatile
Diplomatic	Pioneering	Vigorous

It's also useful to think about your overall preferred approach to work. For example, are you someone who wants to be a specialist within a niche or technical area, or do you prefer to have a more generalist role, using a broad skill-set? Also, are you someone who wants to be able to get on with making their own contribution, or do you yearn for some management responsibility?

This latter question is a particularly important one: there's a general assumption in the corporate world that your career progression should be upwards, which usually means a move into management. But this doesn't suit everyone and there's no reason why you should assume that your career should take the traditional path. Career progression for you might mean developing your niche or specialism, allowing you to stay closely involved in the issues that really interest you. Indeed, companies risk losing some of their best employees if they fail to recognise that success does not always mean moving upwards.

It's important to be clear about the way in which you want to work, not only to help you choose the right role in the first place, but also so that, as your career develops, you are in a much stronger position to resist pressure from your employer to move into roles to which you are less well suited.

Other people's perspectives

Once you've compiled a first draft of your skills, strengths and style lists, it's time to get some feedback from other people. Ask half a dozen of your friends and family, and work colleagues if you can, to list five words that come to mind when they think of you, and to list what they see as your top five skills. Clients often dread this exercise, but it's really useful, and the feedback will not be anything like as bad as you think! What you should be looking out for are words or themes that crop up consistently across different people's responses. These are clear indications of what other people see as your core characteristics and skills. With luck, they should be broadly in line with your own skills, strengths and style analysis, but most people get the odd surprise. In fact, this exercise can be especially useful in helping to identify 'unseen skills': those that you take for granted because you use them often or without thinking about them too much.

Pulling it all together: your 'brand'

By this stage you should have a much clearer idea of your favourite skills, your key strengths and your preferred working style, as well as some feedback from other people that should help to highlight particularly strong characteristics. What you need to recognise is that *your* combination of skills, strengths and style is unique to *you*. No one else will have exactly the same package. Your personal blend of the skills you enjoy and the way in which you like to work makes up your professional **brand**.

It's well worth taking some time to refine the description of your brand. Ask yourself which of your key skills and strengths are most important to you. Ask yourself what really makes you different. What do you bring to the party? What is it about you that makes you stand out? What do you want to be remembered for?

Now write a one-paragraph description of your brand. You'll probably need more than one go at this, but start with an initial draft and keep refining it. This paragraph is the template against which you should assess every career or job opportunity. It's also the basis for every CV you will submit.

If you've given these exercises the time and attention they deserve, you should now have a very clear idea of what you have to offer, the skills you want to incorporate in your career and your operating style. Next, we're going to look at the other key building block for effective career planning: your interests.

Chapter 4

Your Interests

In this chapter we're going to focus on your interests, because they are the key pointers to the fields or industry sectors that are likely to suit you best. The rationale for this is quite simple: you need to be genuinely interested in what you're doing if you want to enjoy your work and be really successful at it. The activities that you do or take part in in your spare time have one very important factor in common: you choose to do them because they interest you and you enjoy them.

I'm not necessarily suggesting that your hobby should become your job, although for lots of people that's a great route to career satisfaction: check out some of the case studies at the end of the book for some examples. But what I am saying is that the subjects and activities that naturally appeal to you and engage you are the best starting point for considering your career options. A satisfying career will be yours if you are using the skills you love to use, in an environment that naturally interests you. Some people – especially those with wide-ranging interests and a natural sense of curiosity – can get interested in almost any field, but for most of us there's a much smaller range of issues and subject matter that appeals to us. In Chapter 6 I'll show you how to use your interests audit to identify industry sectors likely to suit you, but first you need to identify those interests!

Start by answering these questions:

- How do you spend your spare time? What do you do at weekends and on holiday?
- What would you like to have more time to do?
- What do you like talking about? (On which topic could you talk for Britain, or bore your friends almost to death? If you had to give a five-minute presentation on any subject under the sun, what would your topic be?)
- What do you like reading about? (Which newspapers and magazines do you subscribe to or buy regularly? If you buy a weekend paper, which parts do you always read in detail and which sections go straight in the bin? Which articles catch your eye?)
- What sort of non-fiction books do you read?
- What do you watch on television?
- What do you like learning about? If you could take a course just for fun, what would you study?
- If you wrote a book, what would it be about?
- Are there issues or campaigns that you are passionate about? (Environmental

issues, breast cancer, the war in Iraq, human rights, education, science?)
- What hobbies did you pursue when you were younger? Why did you give them up?
- If you could choose only one of your current hobbies or pastimes, which one would it be?
- If you had a big win on the lottery, how would you spend the rest of your life (once you've had a long holiday)? How would you fill your day if you didn't need to work?

By the time you've answered all these questions, you will have a list of issues and activities that encompasses your interests. Don't leave anything off the list, by the way; if you're really into music or films, for example, don't exclude those on the basis that 'I could never make a career out of that'. Most people think far too narrowly about the options that are open to them; you don't have to be a singer or an actor to have a career in the music or film industry! We'll look at this in more detail later, but for now just make sure that your interests list is as comprehensive as possible.

You might find it helpful to distinguish between two broad types of interest: firstly, interests that are hobbies or pastimes (golf, cookery, film, personal development) and secondly, those that are about issues or campaigns (the environment, equal rights, special educational needs). Both types of interest can be pointers to suitable careers.

Your spare-time activities are also very useful pointers to the kinds of working environment that you might enjoy. Think about the following questions:
- Do you prefer doing things on your own or in a group?
- If you enjoy group activities, how big is the group, and is it made up of people you know well or relative strangers? What kinds of people are they? What role do you play in the group: leader, organiser, secretary or simply team member?
- Do your spare-time activities require generalist or specialist skills?
- How much of your spare time is spent on indoor/outdoor activities?
- How many of your hobbies have a competitive element (team sports, chess, pub quizzes)?

The answers to these questions will help to shed light on the kind of work environment likely to suit you best, and the kind of people you want to work with. We'll come back to these issues in the next chapter, because they're important: aside from the nature of the work you do, the people you work with and the environment you work in are the two factors that have the most impact on your job satisfaction.

By now, if you've been completing the exercises as you go, you should have three key lists:

- your values and priorities;
- your skills, strengths and style; and
- your interests.

The following chapters will take you through how to use this information to identify roles, industry sectors and career paths to suit you. If you feel that one (or more) of your lists is a little lacking in detail, now is the time to go back and spend a bit more time on it (or them); good, detailed information will make the next stage of the career-planning process so much easier.

Chapter 5

Your Ideal Role

Now that you have given some thought to what motivates you, how you like to work and the sorts of tasks that you enjoy, it's time to begin to identify roles that will suit you. In this chapter, you're going to use the information from your values and skills audits to draft your 'ideal role specification'. In other words, you are going to describe your perfect role.

You can do this either in the form of a job description, or a description of your perfect day at work. Some people find the latter more effective, because you can include lots of extra relevant information (for example, what time you get to work, how long your commute is, and so on).

There are two important points to make at the outset. Firstly, what you are trying to do is describe the sorts of tasks that your perfect role would entail. Don't try to give your description a job title; you simply need to focus on what you would be *doing*. In any case, different industries and companies give different names to similar roles, so don't get side-tracked by that at this stage. Secondly, don't worry for now about the type of industry, company or organisation in which you would be carrying out your perfect role; we'll come to that later. Just focus on describing the role itself.

Start by using the information from your **skills** audit to describe the content of the role that would be ideal for you.

1   List the skills that you would be using and the nature of the tasks that you would be carrying out, as well as the proportion of time that you would be spending on each task (for example, 20 per cent of your time making presentations, 40 per cent of your time researching, 30 per cent of your time making/following up new business leads). Remember that your aim is to describe your *perfect* role, so only include tasks you really enjoy, even if you think you are describing a role that doesn't exist!

2   Make sure that the role you describe includes your signature strengths. How would you be using them?

3   Look at what you've written about your personal style and brand, and incorporate that into your description by deciding *how* you would be doing things (for example, would you be making lots of impulsive decisions, or would you be consulting widely with colleagues? Maybe you'd have a high level of autonomy, or perhaps you'd be working in a collaborative way.)

4   Include your thoughts on your overall preferred approach to work: generalist or specialist? Manager or contributor?

Now add in other details that have emerged from your **interests** exercise about the kind of people you would like to work with, and the working environment that you would most enjoy.

Next, look back at your **values** exercise and the list of 'non-negotiables' that you put together: the things you really want to get from your work situation. What do these tell you about the kind of role you are looking for? As we noted in Chapter 2, this list is likely to include practical factors (for example, location, the length of your commute, remuneration and reward) as well as some bigger issues (for example, the company ethos, the amount of autonomy you have in your role, your level of prestige and status). Incorporate all of these in your role description.

Finally, think about the wider context (again, you should refer back to your values exercise here). How do you want your work to fit in with the rest of your life and lifestyle? For example, what sorts of hours do you envisage working? Would you like to work flexibly? Would weekend or shift work suit you, or is 9-to-5 a better option? Include any other factors you have identified in your values/lifestyle exercise that are relevant to the career/work choice that you will make.

By now, you should have a pretty good description of your ideal role or day at work. Don't worry if you feel that there are some gaps: the chances are that you will have identified the elements that are most important for you. Your ideal role specification gives you a template against which to assess a whole range of career options. Working from the bottom-up like this is a much more effective way of identifying good opportunities: if you're not really sure what you're looking for, the temptation is to look at job advertisements and think: 'I *could* do that', rather than asking yourself the key question, which is: 'How much do I *want* to do that?'. Now that you have set out the key elements of your ideal role, you will find it much easier to make a sensible assessment of how well a particular role is likely to suit you.

Of course, you still need to work out the industries or sectors in which you want to carry out your perfect role. That's what we'll cover in Chapter 6.

Chapter 6

Your Ideal Industry

Now that you have an idea of the kind of role that you're looking for, we're going to use the information from your **interests** exercise to draw up a list of industry sectors that might suit you.

As I've explained before, there is a good reason for making your set of interests one of the main building blocks for your career planning. Think how much more engaged you are likely to be in your work if it is in an area that naturally appeals to you, one that you are keen to learn about because you genuinely find it interesting, and that you would probably learn about even if you were not paid to do so!

To take a simple example: let's say that you are an accountant, and you love your role and the tasks that you do (yes, some people do love spreadsheets, bank statement reconciliation and tax returns). But let's say that you're also crazy about football. The chances are you'd much prefer to be an accountant working for your favourite football team, or the Premier League, than an accountant in an NHS hospital or a cosmetics company. Get the idea?

As I've said before, I'm not suggesting that the right route is necessarily to try to turn your hobby into your job, but you do need to be interested in the business that you are in. If you look at people who are at the top of their profession – whatever that might be – what tends to set them apart is that they are passionate about what they do. You can't fake that; the interest and enthusiasm has to be real.

Another point to bear in mind is that, if you are working in an area that genuinely interests you, the chances are that on top of the job satisfaction of your role, there will be perks that come with the job that really appeal to you. This might sound a bit shallow at first, but remember that your remuneration for your work is a complete package, and the perks are part of that. So, to take the example above, free or discounted match tickets are going to be a much better benefit for our football-loving accountant than the cheap lipsticks he might get if he was working for that cosmetics company. A slightly simplistic example, perhaps, but it makes the point.

So, how do you use your interests to find a career? For each of the interests you have listed (for example: sport, music, cooking, politics, environmental issues), you are aiming to identify the industries, organisations and businesses relevant to that interest. This is not as difficult as it sounds, although it will probably take some research.

Most industries have the same broad infrastructure:

- policy/regulatory framework (usually some combination of central and local government and other governing bodies specific to the industry);
- producers/providers of the product/service involved (i.e., the people actually 'doing it'); and
- people who provide services in support of the main industry, for example journalism, marketing, advertising, public relations, finance, sponsorship and legal advice.

As an example, let's say that your main interest is Formula 1 racing. The shape of the industry is something like this:
- **Policy/regulatory framework:** central Government (Department for Culture, Media and Sport) oversees national policy on Formula 1 and related issues (for example, the ban on sponsorship by tobacco companies); the FIA is the industry's own regulatory body.
- **Producers/providers of the product/service:** most obviously the racing drivers themselves, and their teams (such as Ferrari, McLaren and Williams); also the tyre manufacturers (Michelin, Goodwood), the venues and track managers, and so on.
- **People who provide services in support of the main industry:** everything from the event organisers and providers of corporate hospitality, to sponsors, journalists, PR firms, agents, lawyers, TV companies, management teams, PAs... the list goes on.

Let's take another example to help you get the picture. Say you're interested in good food and wellbeing. The key elements of this growing industry are as follows:
- **Policy/regulatory framework:** central Government (Department for Health) oversees national policy on public health and wellbeing (think school dinners, tackling obesity, banning junk food advertising); the Food Standards Agency, the Food and Drink Federation and scores of smaller organisations help to create the regulatory framework as well as make representations to Government on specific issues.
- **Producers/providers of the product/service involved:** restaurants, hotels, chefs, wholesalers, retailers, farmers and other producers.
- **People who provide services in support of the main industry:** nutritionists and dieticians, food critics and writers, advertising and marketing companies, food publications, TV shows, food photographers, publishing companies, public relations firms, lawyers, accountants, and many more.

Using this template, take each of your interests in turn and draw the 'map' of the industry or industries relevant to that interest. Depending on your level of knowledge, you may find that you have to do a fair bit of research at this stage, but it's a good investment: the more you know about the industry, the easier it will be for you to identify suitable opportunities. This research will also enable you to be impressive at interviews, should it come to that. Use a range of resources to help you build up your picture: Google and other search engines are obvious starting points, but also look at relevant publications and the trade press as well as the websites of the industry's professional bodies or trade associations. Seek out people who work in or know about the industry and ask for their perspectives. In particular, keep your eye out for new developments, emerging trends and changes within the industry: as well as giving you ideas for areas in which there could be more opportunities, it's all great interview material.

Take your time on this exercise: your aim is to build up an accurate and detailed picture of your chosen industry sectors, and that will require a bit of effort. But it's definitely time well spent.

Once you have a good picture of the shape of the industry, think about the areas within the industry that are most appealing to you. For example, you might not be interested in the regulatory side of things, but marketing, advertising or public relations might take your fancy. Next, do some more research on the areas that most appeal. How big is this section of the industry? Is it comprised of small independent players, a few large corporates, or a mix? Which companies or organisations seem to be most influential within the industry? Who are the generalists and who are the niche providers?

Repeat this process for all the interests that you have identified. (By the way, as you go through them, you might well decide that you're not interested in getting involved with some of your interests in a professional capacity. That's absolutely fine, but don't make that decision until you've done the research. You could be missing out on a great opportunity!)

Once you've completed this exercise, you have all the tools you need to help you make a good career choice. You know your values and the things you're not prepared to compromise on; you have a picture of your ideal role; and now you have a list of industry sectors and organisations that appeal to you. In Chapter 7 I'm going to show you seven different ways to change career, how to identify which of these approaches is right for you, and how to use the information you've put together about yourself to build your action plan.

Chapter 7

The Seven Ways to Change Career

Now that you have the information you need to manage your career, the next stage is to plan your strategy. There are seven main ways to change your work situation. They are:

1 stay in your current role and organisation, but change the way you do things;
2 stay in your current organisation, but change your role;
3 stay in a similar role, but move to another company within the same industry;
4 stay in a similar role, but move to another company in a different industry;
5 change your role, and move to another company within the same industry;
6 change your role, and move to another company in a different industry; and
7 set up your own business.

In my opinion, '1' is the most straightforward option and '7' is potentially the most difficult, but it's different for everyone. Which option is right for you will depend on how satisfying your current role is, how interested you are in your present industry sector and how much you care about your current employer.

Using what you now know about your values, your skills and your interests, you need to think about what changes you want to make to your role, and whether you really want to change the organisation and/or the industry that you work in. Let's look at each of the seven options in turn, to help you think about the strategy that is likely to suit you best.

Stay in your current role and organisation, but change the way you do things ('Maybe I'm in the right job after all...')

If you picked up this book because you are unhappy, bored or unfulfilled at work, you're probably assuming that that means you're going to have to leave your current job. But your starting point should be to assess your current situation against what you've written about your ideal role and industry sectors. It might well be that your existing role allows you to use many of the skills that you enjoy, that you are interested in the industry you're in, and that it is actually other factors that are causing your dissatisfaction. If you can pinpoint what is making you feel negative about your work, there's a good chance you can do something constructive about it. This is a much less risky option than jumping ship. It makes sense to try to resolve your career dilemmas with the least stress and expense. If you do decide to move on, it's also reassuring to know that you tried everything you could to make things work before bailing out. If what you're really doing is running away from a difficult situation (an autocratic manager or a stressful short-term project, for example), the chances are that you will come up against these problems again in the future, and if you haven't learned how to deal with them, you'll be back to square one.

So start by measuring your current role against your ideal role. How much overlap is there? What proportion of your time do you currently spend using your favourite skills and drawing on your key strengths? Are there ways in which you could tweak or add to your role to incorporate more of these? If your response is 'no', are you sure? Have you discussed the possibilities with your line manager or the human resources department? Think about ways in which you could make your existing role more fulfilling, and talk to your bosses.

Similarly, think about the industry and organisation you're currently in. What attracted you to them in the first place? In particular, what attracted you to the company or organisation as opposed to any of its competitors? Were your assumptions inaccurate in the first place, or has something changed in the meantime? Be as clear as you can about exactly what it is that is the cause of your dissatisfaction; the solutions may be less dramatic than you think. (In Chapter 10, I'll give you lots more strategies and tips for making the most of staying where you are.)

Stay in your current organisation, but change your role ('I love my company but not my job')

This option might be the one for you if you love the company you work for – what they do interests you, you're proud to say you work for them, you enjoy the working environment, for example – but you're feeling bored, unstimulated and unfulfilled on a day-to-day basis.

Have another look at your ideal role specification. Do roles like that exist in your organisation? Could they be created? Which aspects of your ideal role are most important to you, and what openings might be available in your company that would allow you to use more of those skills? Again, the starting point is to have a few conversations. Take the person whose job you'd like to have out to lunch. Ask them how they got their role, what it really involves and where they see themselves progressing from here. You're not trying to poach their job, you're just trying to get a clearer picture of the reality of it.

Obviously, the opportunities for you to change role within your current company will depend on a number of factors, including the size of the organisation, its approach to recruitment and training, and the kind of role that you would like. But savvy employers are keen to hold on to members of staff on whom they have already spent a lot of money in terms of recruitment and training, so it's well worth exploring your options. You'll need to be diplomatic, of course, but if you are keen to stay with the company and can demonstrate your aptitude for a different role, you should be able to make a strong business case. You have some advantages over other candidates for the role you want: you understand the industry and you know the company, its people and how it works. This means that you will be able to concentrate on getting to grips with your new responsibilities, and the chances are you'll know where to turn when there's something that you don't understand. In other words, you're well placed to handle a steep learning curve.

Stay in a similar role, but move to another company within the same industry ('Right job, wrong company')

On the other hand, maybe it's not your role but the organisation that you aren't happy with. You might be in a job that makes good use of your core skills, and in an industry sector that fascinates you, but you're not in love with the company you work for. Perhaps the culture and the working environment don't suit you, or you've realised that everything isn't quite what it was cracked up to be. It might be that there are other companies within the industry that you respect more. The good news is that if you can be very clear about what you don't like about your current company, it makes it much easier for you to identify companies or organisations you *do* want to work for. The trick is to make sure that you do your research thoroughly, so that you know what an organisation is really like, not just what it says it is like!

Stay in a similar role, but move to another company in a different industry ('I just don't care about widgets')

This is likely to be the best option for you if you are in a role that you enjoy – whether that's marketing, finance or whatever – but you're not really interested in what your company actually does. The good news here is that it's not necessarily as difficult as you might think to change industry sectors if you are looking to stay in a similar role. That's because, in carrying out your role you are drawing on your key skills and attributes; these are things you already possess, and you should be able to demonstrate them. Knowledge of a new industry sector is something that you can learn, both while you are researching job options and preparing for interviews, and subsequently on the job. The key thing in this situation is to be able to show that you have the right *aptitude* and *attitude*: in other words, that you not only have the relevant skills as a result of performing a similar role, but you have the ability to learn about your new industry quickly, and you have the passion for it. Enthusiasm and hunger to learn are two of the most attractive attributes that any job candidate can demonstrate.

One of the difficulties that you might find if you are this situation, however, is getting recruitment agencies to take you seriously. That's because they're usually trying to find the candidates who are the most obvious fit, and so are more likely to favour those with experience of the industry in question. All is not lost, however, and later in the book I'll show you not only how to deal with agencies, but also lots of other (probably more effective) ways of conducting your job search.

Change your role, and move to another company within the same industry ('I want to do something else with widgets')

This could be your situation if you are still passionate about the industry sector that you work in, but you're ready for a change of role. Perhaps you like your current company but for some reason they aren't able to offer you the job you'd really like (for example, they're too small; there just isn't a vacancy; or they don't specialise in that area), so changing employer is the only option. Or the problem might be two-fold: not only are you in the wrong role, but the organisation you're currently with doesn't value the things that you do, or let you work in the way that suits you best.

In a case like this, you need to emphasise two things to maximise your chances of getting the job you want. Firstly, your detailed knowledge of the industry sector, including specific knowledge of the company you want to work for. (In any case, if you are looking to change company because where you are isn't a good fit for you, you'll want to research other employers within the industry very thoroughly.) Secondly, you will need to be able to demonstrate how your existing skills and experience qualify you to perform your preferred new role. Many of your skills will be transferable and, if you are focusing on a role that will make use of your best and favourite skills, you should be able to make a convincing case.

Of course, if you are planning to move to a very different role, especially one that is specialist or niche, you might have to consider taking a refresher course, re-training completely or starting again at the bottom. You might feel that you are taking a step backwards, but as part of a longer-term strategy this can be a viable and sensible move. Again, in this kind of situation, it's vital to do some hands-on research, so that you know exactly what you're letting yourself in for. You don't want to spend two years re-training so that you can move from a marketing role to an HR role, only to discover that you hate everything about employment law and personnel policy. (Believe me, this has happened.)

Change your role, and move to another company in a different industry ('Everything about this job sucks')

OK, this is the big one! With (possibly) the exception of setting up your own business (see below), the most difficult career transition is where you are trying to change your role and your industry sector at the same time. It's not impossible by any means, but it's a tough challenge to persuade a prospective employer that you are the best person for the job if you haven't done that kind of role before, and you're new to the industry as well. The key to success in this sort of situation is research and preparation. You need to make a compelling case for your employment, based on the transferability of your skills, your ability to learn quickly and your passion for the job. Again, this is the kind of situation in which the traditional job-search methods (press advertisements, recruitment agencies) are likely to work less well for you, and you'll need to adopt a more creative approach (see Chapter 11).

The other option to consider in this situation is a step-by-step or transitional approach. In other words, instead of trying to get a new role in a new industry all in one go, you could change your role within your current company, and use that as a stepping stone to moving into that role within a new industry. Or do things the other way around: change your industry but not your role, then over time move to your preferred role within your new industry. There are two benefits of this approach: firstly, it's usually more feasible; secondly, it's less risky and considerably less stressful! Have a think about whether it's the role or the industry that is causing you the most dissatisfaction, and decide your strategy accordingly.

Set up your own business ('I just want to do my own thing')

This option deserves a book to itself! This book includes a whole section about setting up on your own, and the bibliography also lists the books and other resources that I have found most helpful in building my own business. At this stage, however, before you get into detailed planning, you simply need to decide whether it's an option that attracts you.

The first thing to think about is whether you are suited to being your own boss. There are different schools of thought here: some experts say that entrepreneurialism requires a particular mindset and personality, others will tell you that anyone is capable of running their own business if they want it enough. Generally, I incline towards the latter view but, that said, I do think there are questions that you need to ask yourself – and answer honestly – before you go down this route. Think about the following:

- How self-disciplined are you? Are you good at working on your own initiative when there's no one there to push you?
- How comfortable are you with the idea of selling yourself (which, whether your business is making and selling a product, or offering a service, is in effect what you will be doing)?
- What's your attitude to risk? Have you got the strength of character to cope with bad times as well as good?
- What's your fallback plan? How would you cope, both practically and emotionally, if your business wasn't a success?

These questions aren't designed to depress you or put you off. But you do need to be realistic about the challenges of being your own boss. Although you can surround yourself with advisers, mentors and a 'support team' – and I strongly recommend that you do – at the end of the day the responsibility for your business's success or failure will be yours and yours alone.

If this is a scenario that excites you rather than fills you with dread, then it really is worth a bit more thought, so turn to Part 4 for more information.

Now that you know the different options available to you, you're in a position to decide which one is likely to work best for you, based on how well your current role, organisation and industry measure up against the ideal roles and industry sectors you have identified. Ultimately, you are likely to decide on one of three broad options:

1   Stay in your current job, but tweak it so that it suits you better. If this is your preferred option at this stage, Chapter 10 will give you ideas on how to go about doing this.
2   Change job or career. If you're thinking along these lines, Part 2 of this book will guide you through the job-search process.
3   Set up your own business. If you want to consider this option in more detail, head straight to Part 4.

Chapter 8

Different Ways of Working

As we saw in Chapter 1, the world of work is changing. Perhaps not as quickly or dramatically as some business experts had forecast: the management guru Charles Handy, for example, predicted in the late 1980s that, by the beginning of the 21st century, fewer than half of us would be working in 'proper' full-time jobs. It hasn't quite turned out like that yet, but it's still the case that in the 21st century we have more options open to us than ever before in terms of how we organise our working lives.

Yet most of you reading this book will probably be working on the assumption that your new job will be of the 9-to-5, 40-hours-a-week variety. It doesn't have to be like that. Why not take some time to think in a bit more depth about the working pattern that is best for you, and that fits best with your values and lifestyle choices? This chapter sets out some options to get you thinking, and outlines their pros and cons. Some of these approaches can also be useful as ways of helping you to make the transition to the job you really want: by freeing up time for your proper job search, giving you an opportunity to have a taste of different careers, or giving you a chance to experiment with your business idea. But they are just as valid as long-term career options in themselves, as some of the case studies at the end of this book show.

'Portfolio' working

The idea of a 'portfolio' or 'freestyle' career is one that does seem to be gaining currency. The premise is that, instead of having one full-time job, you make your living through two (or more) part-time jobs. This can be a good approach for people who have a wide range of interests and get bored easily (you could have two quite different jobs). Equally, sometimes it is possible to organise things so that you achieve synergy between your two jobs (that is, so that they add value to each other). For example, you might work a couple of days a week for a PR agency, and spend the rest of the time running your own life-coaching business. The contacts you make through your work with the PR agency could help you publicise your business.

Advantages

1   You have a more interesting range of work.
2   If you're setting up your own business, this can be a good way of

supplementing your income while you build up your client base (it does, though, depend on the nature of your business, which might require your full-time attention).

3   If you're in the early stages of your career, this can be a good way of trying out different kinds of work, to build up experience on your CV, and see what suits you best.

4   Sometimes it can be easier to earn more by working two or three days a week in two different jobs than full-time in one job.

Disadvantages

1   You might end up earning less money.
2   It can be difficult to juggle two jobs, so you'll need to be ultra-organised.
3   You might end up working more hours than you wanted to.
4   You'll find it harder to explain to people what you do!

Part-time working

Who says you have to work full-time? Of course, there are financial considerations to be taken into account, but many people decide that the pay-off for having less money (more time, less stress, more freedom) is worth it. It all comes down to what is most important to you, and that's something only you can decide.

Advantages

1   You have more time for yourself.
2   You might have some flexibility in the hours/days you work.
3   Part-time working can be a good transitional position, as it gives you the time to conduct a proper job search.
4   Many smaller companies are attracted to part-time workers, as they might not be able to afford to employ someone full-time.

Disadvantages

1   You will earn less money.
2   You might feel less engaged with your company/organisation.
3   Your boss and fellow employees might still expect you to do five days' work in three, because there's no one to deal with your in-tray on the days you're not there.
4   Some people – both at work and outside it – won't take you seriously enough.

Compressed hours

This is a slight variation on part-time working, but without the financial drawbacks. Basically, if you are contracted to work a 40-hour week, you agree with your employer that you can work those 40 hours in four days. So, for example, you work from 8am through to 6pm from Monday to Thursday, and have Fridays off.

Advantages

1 You have more time for yourself.
2 You don't lose out financially.
3 Particularly if you have a long commute to work, this can be an efficient way of organising your working week.

Disadvantages

1 Not every company will feel able to accommodate this style of working (although you've got nothing to lose by asking!).
2 You might still need to be available to deal with urgent enquiries on your day off.
4 You might be knackered by Friday!

Flexi-working

Like working compressed hours, this approach gives you more say over how and when you work your contracted hours. For example, you might work from home one day a week, or come in to the office early and leave early.

Advantages

1 It's easier to fit your professional life around other priorities, such as children or a hobby.
2 If you are a commuter, you can miss out on rush hour and often get cheaper travel too.
3 Again, you don't lose out financially.

Disadvantages

1 Not every company or organisation can, or is willing to, operate a flexitime scheme.
2 Colleagues might resent the fact that you leave early (even though you're in the office before them in the morning) if they have to field calls for you once you've gone.

Project work/freelancing

Depending on the industry, project working on a contract or freelance basis can be a viable option. It does suit some industries (for example, IT, marketing, events or sales) better than others; but there's a demand for interim project managers or contract workers in lots of different areas, so it's worth exploring, especially if you like the idea of working on a time-on, time-off basis.

Advantages

1 Lots of flexibility, which is great if (for example) you like to do a lot of travelling.

2   Lots of variety in your work.
3   Rates of pay can be higher than for full-time employment in the same industry.
4   It's an approach that works well for both large and small companies, so there's often plenty of opportunity.

Disadvantages

1   You need to be able to cope with the uncertainty of not knowing where your next job is coming from.
2   Your income stream might be quite erratic, so you'll need to be good at budgeting.
3   When you're on a project, you might be working long hours.
4   You need to get very good at marketing yourself.

The point of this chapter is to encourage you to think beyond the traditional working model. Think about what style of working is right for you and how you might be able to achieve that. Don't just settle for a 9-to-5 job without exploring all your options. You might well find another approach that suits you, and your values and lifestyle, much better.

Chapter 9

Thinking that Holds You Back

So, you've decided that you're ready for a change of direction. Good for you! The next section of the book takes you step-by-step through all the strategies you need to adopt and actions you need to take to give yourself the best chance of landing the role you really want. It covers everything from how to write a great CV through to making use of a whole range of job-search strategies. I'll show you how to excel at interview and how to negotiate a good benefits package for yourself. And I won't abandon you at that point: in Part 3 I'll share the secrets of making a great impact in your new role from day one.

First, however, I want to deal with some of the gremlins that people typically face at this stage in the process: the questions, doubts and fears that understandably arise. If they aren't dealt with, these can stop you making the changes you want. Let's look at the things that most commonly hold people back from escaping a job that no longer thrills them, and what you can do about it.

I still don't know what I want to do

What if you've gone through all the exercises in the previous chapters of this book and you *still* don't know what you want to do? The first thing to say is: don't panic. Career change is a big step and it can take time to work out what you really want to do. Try these steps:

● Re-visit your values, skills and interests exercises. Perhaps you've fallen into the trap of rushing these or skimming through the chapters without completing the exercises thoroughly. It's an understandable temptation: you want to see what comes next in the book and get on to your job search as quickly as possible. But if you haven't given the exercises the time and thought they require, you're simply not going to have the information you need to come up with good career options. The bottom line is that, if you've really focused on the exercises, you will have the information you need to make appropriate choices. So your first task is to go back to the beginning and really take the exercises seriously. Take yourself away somewhere for a day and focus on them exclusively. Write down as much as you can in response to every question and exercise. Be as specific and detailed as you can. Then leave it all for a day or two and come back to it with fresh eyes. What themes are emerging?

● Do some more research. Have you explored every aspect of the industry sectors that your interests pointed to? Have you *really*? Get back on the internet, keep reading, get out there and talk to people: the more information you acquire, the greater the chance of your coming across the option you are looking for. Yes, this is time-consuming, and I understand that you just want to get on with getting that new job. But you really need to invest enough time in the research and option-generating process, or you'll simply end up making the wrong move.

- Go to your local bookshop and browse through some career directories. They may well throw up areas you hadn't thought of. Try *Cool Careers for Dummies*, which has a directory of careers that includes lots of off-beat and niche options as well as more mainstream roles. It could spark off a whole range of ideas for you.

- Get some friends together for a brainstorming session. In advance of the session, send them a copy of your exercises. You can edit out some of the more personal stuff if you really want to, but bear in mind that the more information you give people, the higher the chance that they will come up with suitable suggestions. Stick to the rules of a proper brainstorming session: encourage people to put forward any and every idea they think of, make a note of them all, and don't pass judgement on them at this stage. After the brainstorming, sit down by yourself and go through all the notes and suggestions. There'll undoubtedly be ideas you hadn't considered, and suggestions that will in turn lead you to other ideas of your own.

- If you're still completely stuck, see a career coach. Yes, I would say that – but it makes sense. A good career coach will have a wide knowledge of different roles and industry sectors and will be able to look objectively at all your notes and help you generate ideas. If you needed to sort out your finances, you'd go to see an accountant; if you needed to sort out your health, you'd go to see a doctor. Why should it be any different with your career?

I can't pin myself down to one choice

This is another common problem. Especially if you're just starting out in the world of work, the array of choices facing you can be bewildering. How on earth do you narrow yourself down to just one option? This isn't a problem limited to new graduates: many of my clients find that their career search throws up a range of options that would suit them well, and it can be difficult to know which one to choose. Understandably, this is a problem that particularly tends to arise for people who have a wide range of interests and lots of curiosity: lots of different areas appeal to them. There are a number of ways to tackle this problem:

- Give yourself a bit more time before making your final decision. Do even more research into the areas you are considering. Go back to your values and skills exercises. What more can you find out about each of your options that will help you to refine your choice, based on what's likely to be the best match for you?

- Realise that the choice you make now doesn't have to be forever. Most people will change careers more than once during their life, so there's no reason to assume that this career change has to be your last. Obviously, if you're considering a career that will require a considerable amount of time or money for re-training, you'll want to think carefully about how long you're likely to want to stay in that area. Think about which of your options is likely to suit you best at this stage in your life, and which are careers that you could transfer to a number of years down the line if you were still interested. In other words, if you can't put your options in order of preference, try to put them in a logical order of progress.

- Consider a portfolio career (see Chapter 8). Many people believe that a career means working 9-to-5, five days a week for the same company. For many – indeed, most – people, it does, but it doesn't have to. There's no reason why you couldn't have two different jobs, or work four days a week in your main job, leaving you a day a week to pursue other things. This could mean spending time on hobbies that you'll never turn into a career, or giving yourself an opportunity to sample other careers by volunteering or work shadowing, for example. This approach can be especially useful if you can find a synergy between the two roles. For example, you might work part-time for a management consulting company, and spend a day a week working in your own coaching business: your main job could well be a good source of private clients for you. Equally, if you're struggling to find a single role that encompasses all of your key skills and interests, think about splitting your time between two very different jobs. Check out the case studies at the end of the book for some examples of people who have done just that.
- Consider whether there are ways in which you could combine two or more options. For example, if you're interested in public affairs and also in the sports industry, seek out companies or organisations that represent the interests of sporting bodies. Perhaps you're interested in environmental issues, and also in design. What about working for a company that designs or sells environmentally-friendly furniture or workspace solutions?

I'm just not interested in *anything*

This is almost the opposite of the previous problem. I've occasionally encountered clients who get stuck when they come to the interests exercise, because they claim that they haven't got any hobbies or interests. But, trust me, everyone is interested in *something*. Drill down a bit deeper: what do you talk/think/read about? Write down every activity you've done over the past week and think a bit more about what you did and why. Buy the Sunday papers and flick through every section: which parts appeal, what catches your eye, what articles do you read? Force yourself to come up with a list of ten subjects or issues that attracted your interest. Think about what you talked about the last time you met up with friends; which areas of the conversation interested you and which bored you silly? What are your favourite websites? What sort of stuff do you surf on the internet? What do you watch on television? What clues does all of this give you? Observe yourself for a week and write down everything that you see, read or talk about that interests you in any way. Use this list as your starting point for thinking about industries.

I want to do something trivial

The short answer to this one is: there's no such thing as a trivial job. I often meet clients who know what they want to do, but are almost embarrassed to admit it because they feel they should be doing something 'worthy'. One client really wanted to open a perfume shop; another wanted to be an interior designer; yet another wanted to publish cookery books. The thing that was holding them all back was that they worried that these pursuits weren't important. My response to them – and to you if this is your situation – is this: the only thing that matters is that your job should be important to *you*. If you are in the role that is right for you, you are making a bigger contribution in two ways. Firstly, because you are happy and professionally fulfilled, you will be a much nicer person to be around, and will have a lot more emotional energy to support the people you care about. Secondly, as I've said, no job is trivial. To take the examples I listed above, think of the pleasure that a lovely scent brings, whether you're treating yourself or buying it as a gift. Think of how much more relaxed and positive you would be if your home was a beautifully decorated, well-organised haven; think of the pleasure of a lovely meal shared with friends. First and foremost, your work is about you and the level of fulfilment and purpose that it gives you. We can't all save the world – in fact, none of us on our own can save the world – but we can all make our contribution in our own way.

Other people don't approve of my choice

This is a common problem: many people find themselves holding back from making a career change because of their fears about other people's reactions. However, it's important to distinguish between *emotional* and *practical* issues here. As an example, if you've got a mortgage to pay and a family to support, it simply might not be practical for you to stop working and go off to re-train. This is very different from avoiding changes because you are worried that other people will be critical of your decision. But there are effective ways of handling both types of situation.

If you have a partner, children or other people who are dependent on you, your proposed career move is going to impact on them in some way. If you are looking to change career completely, there is likely to be some financial impact: maybe you will need to take a drop in salary for a while, or perhaps your transition plan means that you will be working part-time while you build up your own business or undertake some training. Even if your job change won't involve a reduction in income (for example, if you're simply seeking to move to another company within your current industry), those around you will still be affected by the time you have to devote to your job search and the stress that you are likely to experience at some point in the process. Whatever the situation, you need to agree a practical plan that works for everyone involved.

Set aside some time when you can sit down with your partner (or whoever is going to be affected), and try to work together to come up with a sensible plan. Issues to discuss include:

- What will be the likely impact on your lifestyle of your proposed career move? For example, will you need to relocate? Will your journey to work take longer? Will you be working longer or different hours?
- What are the financial implications and how will you manage them? If it's likely that you will have to take a salary cut, at least in the first instance, how can you budget for that?
- What impact will the job-hunting process have on the amount of time you have available for other things? What support can your partner give you in the short term? For example, would he or she be prepared to take on more childcare or other domestic tasks to give you more time for research or networking?

It's important to be clear about all these issues from the outset, as there's little point in embarking on a career change only to discover halfway through that it isn't feasible for financial or other practical reasons. I'm going to be realistic here: you may well find that you need to reach a compromise. For example, instead of chucking in your job straightaway to concentrate on setting up your own business (which I wouldn't advise anyway unless you have a significant financial buffer), you might need to keep working full- or at least part-time and build up your business in the evenings and at weekends. Or, if you live in Norwich but the company you really want to work for is based in London, you'll need to decide whether to move the whole family to London, to commute to London every day, or to stay in London during the week and go home at weekends. Or maybe there's a company nearer to home where you could find a job similar to the one in London. The important thing is to find a solution that works both for you and for those who will be affected by the change. It can be useful, as part of this process, to revisit your values exercise. What are the things that are most important to you, and how can you reflect those in the plan that you make? Which issues are you prepared to compromise on, and which are your non-negotiables? Enlist your partner's help in working out the right trade-offs.

What do you do if your partner is totally opposed to your career change? Try to get them to spell out exactly what their concerns are. They love you (at least, I'm assuming they do!) and they want you to be happy, but that doesn't mean that their worries aren't justified. Perhaps they are concerned that you won't have as much time for them, or that finances will be too tight, or that you haven't thought your choices through carefully enough and will simply end up exchanging one inappropriate job for another, only to go through the whole process again a couple of years later. Take their objections seriously: they might well have legitimate concerns that you have overlooked in your eagerness to make changes. Again, try to work together to come up with a solution or compromise that works for both (or all) of you.

Of course, you might be young, free and single with no commitments, or you might have enough financial flexibility to make a career change without it significantly affecting your lifestyle. But you will still have to deal with the emotional issues around your change of direction. For many people, the biggest stumbling block is: 'What will other people think?' Perhaps you want to do something that your parents think is risky or not professional enough. Maybe you're worried that your friends will think you're mad. Or perhaps part of you can't help thinking that your current colleagues will believe that you are selling out, or walking away because you can't cope.

The only way to deal with these worries is to trust your own judgement. You are the person who knows you best, so you are best placed to make the choice that's right for you. If you've carried out the analysis, the research and the planning that this book advises, you're highly unlikely to make a rash or unsuitable decision. Remind yourself of your priorities: what's really important to you? Other people have different perspectives and goals, so you can't expect them necessarily to share your dreams. Accept responsibility for your own life. Other people's opinions are just that – opinions. Only you know what you really want to achieve.

I can't afford it

This is – for understandable reasons – one of the most common objections that people raise as to why they can't make the career change that they say they want. Equally, I think this is often an excuse, rather than a reason, for not taking action. If you want to make change badly enough, you'll find a way of affording it. Cut your spending, save really hard for a year (or however long it takes), find a way of 'transitioning' into your new career so that you don't have to take too heavy a financial hit. Of course, the more responsibilities you have – mortgage, kids, dependants – the harder it will be, but there's nearly always a way.

I had a client a while ago whose lifelong dream was to become a pilot for a commercial airline. It's a very competitive field, with only a few sponsored places available. The alternative is to pay for your own training, which costs around £60,000. Perhaps understandably, my client said that he just couldn't afford that. But I think that if he had wanted his dream enough, he could have found a way. Even if he'd had to borrow the money, the high salary he'd earn when he qualified would have meant that he could pay off the debt relatively quickly. Instead, he's sacrificed his dream and settled for a job he doesn't enjoy. He's only just 30, so he's got a lot of unfulfilled career ahead of him. It all boils down to how much you want something, and what trade-offs you are prepared to make to get it.

What if I fail?

Fear of failure is another big stumbling block for many people. As we'll see in Chapter 17, the ability to deal with failure is one of the attributes that sets successful people apart. One way to look at it is to tell yourself that staying where you are, instead of having a go at what you really want to achieve, is much more of a failing than trying to make a change, even if it doesn't turn out quite how you expected. You'll always have regrets if you don't have a go. Get things in perspective: what's absolutely the worst thing that could happen, and how would you handle it? Once you know that you can deal even with a worst-case scenario, there's much less to be afraid of. Use your fear as a positive emotion to help you focus and give your best, rather than a negative one that stops you having a go in the first place.

I just keep putting it off

Possibly the single biggest reason why people don't achieve their dreams is that they never get round to taking the first step. A while ago I read Sahar Hashemi's book *Anyone Can Do It*, which tells how she had an idea for New York-style coffee bars in London, and how she and her brother started Coffee Republic literally at their kitchen table. Sahar relates how, after Coffee Republic had become hugely successful, people would often approach her and say 'Yeah, we had an idea for coffee bars just like yours'. Her response was: 'Yes, but the difference between you and me is that I got out there and did it!' That's exactly the point: the difference between successful people and people who never get beyond their pipe dream is that successful people get out there and get on with it.

What stops us taking action? We put things off for lots of different reasons: maybe we're scared, or we don't know where to start, or we don't want to make mistakes so we don't do anything. Procrastination is such a big stumbling block for so many people that I've included a whole chapter on it in this book. So if you're procrastinating, don't put it off: read Chapter 19 now!

Part 2

Landing Your Perfect Job

Chapter 10

Making the Most of Where You Are

In Chapter 7, we saw that one of the most straightforward and least risky ways of changing job is not to change job at all! If you've been reading this book because you're not happy at work (and why else would you?), then the idea that the best option for you might be to stay where you are could make you feel a bit disappointed. Perhaps you've been hoping for an exciting revelation or flash of inspiration about your new career. Well, sometimes that inspiration can come from somewhere close to home.

As I stressed in Chapter 7, I firmly believe that anyone considering a career change should look carefully at their current situation first. As we have seen, there are a number of reasons for this.

- Your current role might, with a bit of tweaking, allow you to use more of your preferred skills and strengths in an industry you already know (which means you have many of the tools for a successful career already in place).
- There is always a risk in changing careers. If your current job isn't making you happy, the chances are that you can find something that suits you better, but there's no guarantee of that. This is especially the case if your current job actually measures up quite closely to your ideal role and industry. That indicates that the problem lies elsewhere; maybe you need to focus on some other issues that might be the cause of your dissatisfaction, such as your pay and conditions, or your relationship with colleagues.
- You should make very sure that you are not simply running away from problems that you need to learn to resolve, such as communicating better or managing your time more effectively. Be honest with yourself: are there areas of your performance that are letting you down? If so, I suggest that you think about trying to improve on these areas before you move on. (I know I have said that you should concentrate on your strengths and not your weaknesses, and I believe that. But there are some skills that you can't afford to be deficient in if you want your career to go places.)
- Changing career can be expensive, stressful and risky. If you do decide to go ahead with a career move, this book will show you how to minimise the risks, the stress and the expense, and get the best result possible. But don't change

career just for change's sake; make sure that you are clear about why your current career isn't working, and that you have explored all the possible options to fix your current situation.

Can you make it work?

Try to pinpoint as precisely as you can the reasons why you are unhappy in your current situation. Be brutally honest; this is for your eyes only. Below are some factors that commonly affect people's job satisfaction levels and that can often, if not always, be resolved through communication and maybe a bit of lateral thinking.

Disliking your boss, colleagues or customers

Not getting on with the boss is one of the most common reasons for people leaving their jobs. This makes sense: your manager is likely to be the person who has the biggest impact on your work and your enjoyment of it, so if your relationship with him or her is poor, it's bound to affect your job satisfaction. Similarly, if you don't get on with the people you spend most time with at work, whether they are clients or colleagues, you're likely to be miserable. The first thing to do in this situation is: make sure the problem isn't you. Are you friendly, courteous, professional and polite at all times? Or could there be aspects of your approach that rub other people up the wrong way? Maybe you can be a little brusque, or negative, or just not very communicative? No one is saying that you have to be best friends with everyone at work, but a positive and approachable attitude is important. If, on the other hand, you get on well with most people but there's one person who's making your life a misery, then you need to take action. If that person is your boss it can be tricky, but unless they are an out-and-out bully (in which case there's probably not a lot you can do except get away from them), the chances are that they aren't aware of the effect their behaviour is having. Perhaps they don't involve you in decisions, or never give you any feedback on your work. The key is communication; ask for a meeting and explain, gently and positively, how you would like to be more involved, would appreciate more feedback, or whatever. Similarly, if it's a colleague whose behaviour is upsetting you, consider a quiet, polite word with them and, if that fails, think about raising the issue – in confidence – with your line manager. At the end of the day, however, if you just can't get on with the people you work with, it might be time to move on, perhaps to another role or department within the organisation. Don't assume that the answer is necessarily to jump ship completely. Whatever move you make, though, do make sure that it's not your own attitude that is at fault, otherwise the same problems will simply arise all over again.

Stress and overwork

This is another biggie. More and more of us are finding our workloads increasing and more demands being placed on us. Again, the first response in this situation should be to talk to the people who might be able to help, whether that's your manager or the HR department. Put together your case in advance, including: the evidence that you have too much on your plate; how you propose the situation could be resolved (by hiring a temp or an intern, perhaps); and the benefits to the organisation (fewer errors and quicker turnaround times, for example). Also, look at your own processes and time management. Are there tasks on which you could spend less time? Do you have appropriate systems in place? Are you clear about your work priorities and do you focus your time on them? We'll look at the issue of time management in Chapter 18, and it's well worth investing in one or two of the specialist books listed in the bibliography, as there are lots of ways in which you can streamline your work processes, which in turn helps you to manage your workload and reduce your stress levels. That said, these techniques will only help if your workload is actually manageable in the first place. If you are constantly swamped and exhausted but unable to switch off from work, and especially if it's starting to affect your health or relationships, then you should think seriously about moving on.

Pay and other rewards
Ask someone to name the most important factor in job satisfaction and the chances are they will say 'money'. But, in fact, for most people, salary is what is known as a 'hygiene' factor: as long as you are being paid a fair rate for the work you do, money is unlikely to be a significant motivator. Instead, research has shown that being appreciated and feeling part of things are stronger drivers than salary and job security. And of course your pay is only part of the whole reward package; other elements such as flexitime, generous annual leave or a good pension scheme need to be factored in to the overall equation. That said, if you feel that you are underpaid, it is likely to have a negative effect on your motivation and performance. And, in any case, you owe it to yourself to ensure that you are being paid what you are worth. Most of us hate the idea of negotiating over pay. For some reason, we find it embarrassing to have to try to sell or justify ourselves in blunt monetary terms. But if you're not happy with your pay, you're not going to be happy in your job, so you need to tackle this problem.

Six must-dos when asking for a payrise
1   Do your research. What's the market rate for your job? Check out job advertisements or talk to a friendly recruitment consultant to discover the going rate.
2   Schedule a time with your boss and think through what you'll say, but try to keep the meeting as normal as possible. Don't build it into a crisis situation. Stay calm and positive.

3　Make your case. List your contributions and achievements, quantifying where possible ('I've exceeded targets by X per cent this year').
4　If asking for more money feels too stressful, imagine you're asking on behalf of a friend. How would you put their case? This technique helps you distance yourself and be less emotionally involved.
5　Think flexibly. What are your motivations? Is it just about money? Would you accept an extra day's holiday/flexible hours/a day each week working from home in lieu of more money?
6　What's your fall-back position? What's the minimum rise you'll accept, and what other options do you have if your manager says 'no'? Decide what you will/won't be happy with before you go in.

Lack of prospects

Feeling stuck in a job with no obvious prospects of promotion can be a very demotivating experience. With many organisations adopting flatter management structures, it is also increasingly common. So what do you do when you feel ready to take the next step on the ladder, but there aren't any opportunities available? Think about other ways in which you can stretch yourself and continue to develop. Talk to your manager about the possibility of taking on a special project, extending your area of responsibility, or maybe making a sideways move so that you have the chance to learn about a different area of the organisation. Think about ways in which you could add value to the company as well as to your CV. For example, you could get involved in the organisation's mentoring scheme for new staff, or start one up if there isn't one in place already. Do make an effort to explore all your options for professional development within your existing organisation before deciding to move on. Give your employers the opportunity to show that they value you.

Time to move on?

The problems above are issues that can often be resolved with a bit of work and imagination. If you're otherwise happy at work – if you respect your employer and are interested in what you do – it's worth making the effort to find solutions. The common theme of the problems listed above is that you have some scope to influence the situation. But there are situations in which moving on could well be your best option. Some issues are simply too difficult, if not impossible, to resolve. Let's have a look at some of them.

Culture or values clash

If your values are at odds with the company culture, you're probably going to find it very difficult to get real satisfaction from your job. As we saw in Chapter 2, your values are the fundamental building blocks for your career, and it's vital that you take them into account. Whether you are uneasy about the organisation's ethics, or you've found that the company is very bureaucratic and process-driven whereas you work better in a less structured environment, if it's not a situation that you can fix you should move on. The good news is that, now you are much more aware of your values and your non-negotiables, you'll be much more likely next time around to select a work culture and environment that suits you.

'I just don't care about it anymore'

It's not uncommon to lose interest in something that once excited you. That's why many people have several careers throughout their working life: they simply get to a point where they're no longer passionate enough about what they're doing to make it worthwhile getting out of bed in the morning. This is particularly the case, I've found, for people with a wide range of interests, a high level of natural curiosity and a low boredom threshold. Once they've got a general grasp of their subject area, they're ready to move on to something else. There's nothing wrong with this approach at all, although you need to make sure that you don't job-hop so frequently that you begin to look as though you have no staying power. Once you've lost interest in or become bored by a subject, it's hard to rekindle your enthusiasm, so it's probably time to look elsewhere.

Changes in personal circumstances

Sometimes the factors that mean your job just doesn't work for you any more are personal. For example, you (or your partner!) have just had a baby and you no longer want to spend weeks of the year abroad on business. Or you might decide that you want more flexibility in your working hours, or to take a career break or sabbatical, but these aren't viable options in your current role. It's always advisable to have a chat with your manager or HR department if your personal situation changes: if the company has spent time and money training you, your managers might well be keen to help you find ways of managing your new personal circumstances and staying in your job. But, ultimately, your work is only one part of your life, and it's often one of the more straightforward areas in which to make adjustments. So if your personal circumstances change, it's sensible to look at how you can alter your work to accommodate that.

It's just no fun anymore

If you've not been enjoying your job for some time, and you've explored all the 'tweaking' options that I've suggested above, then it probably is time to move on. Life is too short, and we spend too much of it at work, to put up with a job that makes you miserable. The key thing to be aware of in helping you to plan your next step is exactly why you're not enjoying it anymore. Be as specific as you can; for one thing, you'll need to explain your reasons for moving to recruiters and potential employers but, more importantly, you need to use this information to help you get the right job next time round.

If any of these situations applies to you, you probably do need to change jobs. But if you are still interested in your industry, you respect your employer, there is scope for you to adapt your role to suit you better or to tackle your key frustrations, then it's probably worth another shot.

One final thought: if you've looked at your options and decided to stick with your current employer, it's useful to regard this renewed commitment as a bit of a fresh start. Part 3 of this book looks at strategies and tips to help you make an impact in a new job. You can use the approaches suggested there to help you raise your game, refresh your approach and put your career on the fast-track.

Chapter 11

Job-search Strategies

If you've got this far, I'm guessing that you've come to the conclusion that you can't make your current job work for you, and you need to move on. If so, you have a range of options, as we saw in Chapter 7:
- change your role but stay in the same industry;
- stay in the same role but change industry;
- change both role and industry; or
- set up your own business.

If you've decided that you want to stay in the world of employment (as opposed to self-employment), this chapter guides you through the strategies and tactics you need to adopt to give you the best chance of landing the job you want. If you've done the exercises in Part 1, you should have a clear idea of the kind of role you're looking for, and the industry you want to work in: this chapter gives you the tools you need to make it happen.

There is a whole range of different approaches to job-hunting. In what I believe is roughly their order of effectiveness (the first being the most effective; the order might surprise you), they include:
- networking;
- speculative applications;
- responding to advertisements (whether in print or online); and
- headhunters and recruitment agencies.

This chapter covers each approach in turn. The best job search will include most, if not all, of these elements, but some approaches are more useful than others, depending on your specific situation. For example, recruitment consultants are more useful if you are planning to move company but stay within the same industry, whereas if you are looking to change industry then networking is likely to be more effective. Whichever approach or combination of approaches you adopt, there are a few key strategic points that are well worth remembering.

Treat your job search as a job in itself

If you are going to get results, you really need to give your job search proper time and attention. In some ways this is easier if you are not currently working (although issues like procrastination and making sure you use your time effectively are relevant whether or not you're working). However, most people plan their next career move while they are still in their current job. If that's the situation you're in, you will need to be disciplined about carving out time in your diary, otherwise it will simply never happen. Think of this as a project for which you are the project manager; although other people such as networking contacts, friends and family, and even a career coach, can help you, the responsibility for achieving your desired outcome is yours and yours alone.

Use your time effectively
Given that your time for career planning is likely to be limited, it follows that you need to use that time effectively. That means that you need to spend your time on the activities that are most likely to get you results. As a broad rule of thumb, I'd say that means spending about 60 per cent of your time on networking, 20 per cent on speculative applications and 20 per cent on responding to online or print advertisements and dealing with recruitment agencies. Your efforts also need to be targeted; as we'll see in more detail below, less is often better than more. A focused, targeted job search is much more likely to generate results than a scattergun approach. Chapter 18 gives some more general advice on time management, which is as relevant to your job search as it is to your effectiveness in your new workplace.

Focus, focus, focus
Be very clear what you're looking for. Re-visit your values exercise and your list of non-negotiables. Look again at your ideal role and ideal industry/organisation list. Use these checklists ruthlessly to screen out jobs that don't meet enough of your criteria, and to help you target your networking and make the best use of your – and your contacts' – time.

Think about the employer's perspective
When it comes to recruitment, employers are risk-averse. For many reasons employers dislike having to advertise a job; it's expensive, it's time-consuming to sift through what might be hundreds of applications, and getting the right person at the end of the process is a bit like finding a needle in a haystack. That's why, when they're looking to fill a vacancy, most employers prefer to seek out someone they already know who would be suitable for the post or someone who has been referred to them by someone whose judgement they trust. Failing that, they might well consider unsolicited (but suitable) applications (which saves them the time, expense and effort of the recruitment process), or hand the job over to headhunters or recruitment consultants (which at least saves them some time, if not expense). When you look at the recruitment process from the employer's perspective, therefore, you can see why job-search techniques such as networking and speculative applications are likely to be much more effective than you might initially think.

Remember that the job market can be a jungle
People won't always be nice to you. If you make a speculative application, it might

not be acknowledged. If you call someone up to ask for a moment of their time, they might say 'no'. You might submit your CV to a recruitment agency and never hear back from them. Finding the right job takes diligence, focus, effort and time, and sometimes you need to have a thick skin. Changing job is one of the most stressful things you can do; it's up there with bereavement, divorce and moving house. I don't say all of this to make you feel despondent. With perseverance, you will get there. But it's sensible to recognise that there will be times when you feel that you are hitting your head against a brick wall, or getting nowhere. In these situations, you need to change your strategy or tactics if necessary, but keep going and don't give up.

Having given you these pointers and warnings, let's look in some more detail at the job-search choices that you have.

Job-search strategies

Networking

For the reasons I've explained above, I honestly believe that this is one of the most effective job-hunting approaches. Yet most people instinctively shy away from it. Why? Probably for some, or all, of these reasons:

1   they think it's pushy and artificial;
2   they're afraid they'll be rejected or embarrassed;
3   they think it's too time-consuming; and/or
4   they don't know how to go about it.

Each of these objections is understandable, but they're all flawed. Let's consider them in turn.

'Networking is pushy and artificial'

Yes, it is, if your approach is to try to meet as many new people as you can, push your business card on to them and ask them for a job straight out! The secret of successful networking is to recognise that it's a medium-term, not a short-term, game; that it's about building lasting relationships; and that it's a reciprocal arrangement – it's about giving as well as receiving. Networking is about increasing your 'reach' (or building your 'personal web', as careers writer John Lees describes it), and it's about learning (about people, about the industry that interests you, sometimes even about yourself).

'What if I'm rejected or made to feel embarrassed?'

Again, if you handle things the right way, this is unlikely to happen. Your approach in networking is never to come straight out and ask for a job. What you are seeking is information: what can the person tell you about the industry? How did they get to where they are? Do they have helpful comments to make on your

CV or work history? Can they recommend other people to whom you could speak to find out more, or who might be able to help you with job opportunities? Most people are flattered to be asked for their advice, and are happy to talk about their own experiences. If you bear these two facts in mind, and tailor your approach accordingly, you will find that few people reject your request for help.

'It's too time-consuming'
Well, first of all, it doesn't have to be. If you start with people whom you already know or come into contact with (see below), then it can simply be a part of your existing activities. If you're going to be talking to people anyway, there's no reason why your career can't be one subject of that conversation. Secondly, as we've seen already, effective job-hunting is about using your time well. If networking is more likely to bring you a result than applying to advertised jobs (and it is), then it makes sense to focus your efforts on it.

'I don't know how to go about it'
No problem, just read on!

You might still be asking yourself: if networking isn't a short-term fix, and it's about asking for information not a job, how is it really going to help in my job hunt? The answer to that is: because an effective job-search strategy is all about people and information, the two things that networking provides in spades if it's done properly. The more you know about your chosen industry, and the more people in that industry with whom you can make positive contact, the better your chances of getting your foot in the door.

So how do you go about building up – and making use of – your network? Here are some tips.

Understand the sums
Metcalfe's law states that the value of a community grows as the square of its number of users increases. The law is often quoted as the reason for the rapid growth of the internet, but it applies just as well to personal networks. Put simply, it means that the more people there are in your network, the more possible connections you (and they) have. If you double your number of contacts, you actually quadruple the value of your network.

Start with the people you know
Write down a list of everyone you know, and I mean *everyone*: friends and family, their friends, current and former colleagues, people whose professional services you use (everyone from your accountant to your hairdresser), members of clubs and societies that you belong or used to belong to, people you have met at conferences or other business or social functions. Do this exercise thoroughly and

you're likely to have a pretty long list. And that's just your starting point! You're going to be asking every single one of these people to put you in touch with two or three more contacts of theirs.

Prepare properly

Before you pick up the phone to make initial contact, ensure that you are ready to make a good impression. Be able to describe your current situation and the help that you are seeking concisely and compellingly. The purpose of your phone call in most instances will be to ask for a meeting (obviously it's slightly different when you know the person well; you might arrange to take them for a drink instead, for example). Ask for just 15 to 20 minutes of the person's time; most people will end up giving you more, but don't put them off in the first instance by asking for too much.

Be clear what you are asking for

Once you have arranged a meeting, it is your responsibility to ensure that you make the best use of the time that your contact gives you. You need to be clear about what it is that you want to achieve from your conversation. Make sure that you have done some research into your contact and their organisation, so that you have some initial ideas as to how they might be able to help, or particular aspects of their experience on which you would like them to elaborate. If – as is likely given that you're reading this book – your ultimate aim is to identify job opportunities, then you probably want to ask them for advice on your options, an insider's view of the industry or company you're interested in, and the names of other people with whom they could put you in touch. Remember, you are asking for information, not a job. Most people to whom you speak won't be in a position to give you a job, but they will be able to pass on all sorts of useful information, tips and other contacts.

Don't hog the conversation

When you have managed to secure a meeting – or a telephone call, if the person is too far away – don't spend the whole time talking about yourself. The more you let the other person talk, the more useful information you are likely to gather. That said, if you feel that they are wandering too far from the subject, you may need gently to guide them back on course. But remember, too, that many a good idea or opportunity has arisen from an unexpected turn in the conversation. Whatever else you get out of the conversation, make sure that you do your best to come away with two or more new referrals, and, ideally, the permission of your contact to use his or her name when you introduce yourself to them.

Keep good records

You might think that you'll remember everyone you meet and what they tell you, but trust me, you won't! As well as taking notes during your conversation, keep a record of who you met and when, and to whom they referred you.

Remember the courtesies
Write to thank the person who has spared you some of their time, and make sure that you make contact promptly with anyone they put you in touch with. It won't give a good impression if they find out it's taken you a month to follow up on their suggestion.

Think about what you can give back in return
Networking is a two-way process, so get into the habit of asking yourself what, or whom, you know that might be helpful to your other contacts. Spend time and effort maintaining and building on each of the new relationships that you make. Not only will this help to ensure that your network keeps growing, but it means that, if anyone to whom you have spoken subsequently becomes aware of a suitable opportunity, you are likely to be at the forefront of their mind. It may not be possible for you to keep in regular contact with absolutely everyone that you meet but do, as a minimum, stay in touch with your 'golden contacts' – the people who have given you the most useful information or referrals. Make every effort to give something useful back to them.

Make contact with groups, not just individuals
One way of helping to build your network quickly is to tap into existing groups and networks, so that you have the opportunity to make several contacts in one go. But you need to manage this well; it can be time-consuming, so choose your business networks with care. Where are you most likely to meet people who might be able to help you? Again, don't fall into the trap of thinking that the more business cards you collect at a function, the more productively you have spent your time. Concentrate on having a few genuine conversations rather than rushing around the room trying to say hello to everyone. If those conversations are useful, it's an indication that this is a networking group that it's worth staying involved with. Again, think about what you have to offer, as well as the help that you are looking for.

Speculative applications
As I've made clear, the best way of getting into your company of choice is to network your way in. But if, despite your best efforts, you simply haven't been able to make contact with anyone who works where you want to work, then your next best option is to make a speculative application. This involves contacting the company or organisation for which you want to work, with a view to finding out whether it has any relevant openings. This approach might seem like a bit of a long shot, but you can increase your chances of making it work by being

thorough in your research, and targeting your applications carefully. And remember to look at it from the employer's perspective: if someone has unexpectedly announced their departure, or a manager is thinking about creating a new post, you could just be the answer to their problem. The chances of your letter arriving on their desk at exactly the right moment might be slim, but there's also the chance that they will keep your letter on file for future reference. So, how do you give your speculative application the best chance of success? Here are some top tips.

Make your approach by letter

When you're networking, your first contact is usually a phonecall. It's different with a speculative application. In my experience, the most effective approach is to send a letter in hard copy (not by email). That's because if you try to make contact by telephone, you'll probably find it difficult to get through to the right person. Even if you do, the chances are that they'll be busy, their mind will be on something else, and they will be trying to get you off the phone as soon as possible, so they'll probably just say they have no vacancies. (I should know, I've done it.) This is more likely to happen to you when you're making a cold call about potential vacancies than when you are trying to set up a networking meeting, because you're asking for more (implicitly, if not explicitly, you're asking for a job), and because you don't have the 'hook' of another person's name as an introduction. If your speculative approach is in the form of a letter, however, there's a chance that it will get read and, with any luck, retained. An approach by email might be quicker, but it's all too easy for the recipient to press the 'delete' button, so I recommend the old-fashioned method in this instance.

Do your research

For your unsolicited approach to have the desired impact, you need to get the reader thinking that you could be the solution to their problems. To have a chance of achieving that, you need to know a lot about the company or organisation you are targeting, and the industry within which they operate. What you are looking for is a 'hook' for your letter. For example, if the company has announced that it is expanding, or moving into a new business area, there may well be opportunities, especially if you can demonstrate relevant expertise. Perhaps it's been the subject of a takeover, or maybe a senior manager has moved: new managers can often mean openings for new staff. The national business press, local media and the trade and professional press for the industry are all good sources of this kind of information. Interestingly, job advertisements can also be a good information source; train yourself to read them closely. The post being advertised might indicate wider changes within the organisation, which in turn could mean other opportunities.

Keep your letter punchy

It needs to set out, concisely and compellingly, your understanding of the company and its requirements, and what you have to offer that can add value to its bottom line. And you need to do this in two paragraphs!

Be clear about what you are asking for

Open your letter by making it clear what you are looking for, although do not ask for a job in exactly those terms. Say that you would be keen to discuss ways in which you might be able to make a contribution, or to apply your experience in an organisation/company whose business fascinates you.

Make sure you identify the appropriate recipient

Don't make the mistake of assuming that this is the head of the HR department. You should be aiming to get your letter on the desk of the person who will really benefit from hiring you: your potential boss or, possibly, his or her boss. You can often get this information from the company website; if not, call reception and ask for the name of the person in charge of the functional area in which you are interested. Find out exactly how they should be addressed (for example, if the name you are given is 'Bill Smith', make sure that he isn't known as William to everyone except close colleagues). If the name you are given is that of a woman, find out her preferred form of address (Miss, Mrs or Ms).

Follow up your letter with a phone call

Call a week after you've sent the letter to enquire whether the recipient has had a chance to consider it. Be ready to summarise the content of your letter succinctly; the recipient might not recall it, and might not even have read it! At this point, you should ask for a meeting. If this request is declined (and you need to accept that in many cases it will be), ask for the names of anyone else who might be interested to hear from you. Then say 'thank you' and get off the phone! You don't want to be remembered as a pest or time-waster; you never know whether you will bump into this person again in the future.

Responding to advertisements

This is the tactic that most job-hunters adopt, often to the exclusion of all others. With the growth of online job-search and recruitment services, it's all too easy to spend hours and hours on the web searching for vacancies. But if we remember that the 'hidden' job market (i.e., jobs that aren't advertised) accounts for 80 per cent of vacancies, it's obvious that responding to advertisements should be only a relatively small part of your job-search strategy. Chapter 12 gives more detailed information about how to put together an application that will give you the best possible chance of securing an interview. For now, here are some points to bear in mind.

Scan all the relevant publications regularly

You'll need to keep an eye on the local and national press, as well as publications specific to your industry, which can often be the main advertising medium for vacancies (e.g. *Personnel Today* for the HR industry, *PR Week* for the public relations industry). Local newspapers can be useful if you are looking for jobs in a specific location, and printed advertisements are more often used at a local level. In terms of the national press, different broadsheets tend to specialise in particular industry sectors (e.g., the *Telegraph* for science and engineering jobs), so find out which ones cover your areas of interest, and on which day they publish advertisements or job supplements.

Remember that less is more

A few well-researched and well-written applications will represent time better spent than dashing off responses to anything that looks remotely interesting. Be fussy: if the job specification doesn't meet 70 to 75 per cent of your criteria, don't pursue it. Most advertised roles will attract a flood of applications, and unless your skills and experience are a near-perfect fit, or you can project them as such, you're unlikely to get through the first sift.

Don't apply for an advertised position just to get 'interview practice'

You're just wasting the recruiter's, and your own, time.

Limit yourself to one or two online job-search sites

It's better to register with a couple and check them regularly than to overwhelm yourself with the amount of information that's on the web.

Headhunters and recruitment agencies

I've left this section till (nearly) last because in general, unless you are at a senior level and want to remain in your current industry sector, headhunters (or 'executive search consultants') are unlikely to make a significant contribution to your job-search. Similarly, the extent to which recruitment consultants can help you will be limited unless you are in – and want to stay in – an industry with high demand and relatively high turnover (for example, IT or finance). It's important to understand that both headhunters and recruitment consultants are in the sales business: they make their money from placing candidates (although headhunters are often paid on a retainer basis by large companies, rather than per placement). What this means is that a) they are working for their client (the recruiting organisation), not for you; and b) they are most interested in putting round pegs in round holes. If you are looking to make a significant change either in your role or the sector you work in, don't waste too much time going down the agency route.

That said, around 20 to 30 per cent of jobs are filled through recruitment agencies (more in some sectors, less in others), so don't ignore them completely.

Just make sure that this is only one strand of your job-hunt strategy, and not the main one. Here's how to make the most of what they offer.

Remember that they are not careers advisers
Their business is to put suitable candidates into suitable roles, so if you are looking to make a significant career change, they're unlikely to be too interested.

Headhunters operate by researching and sourcing likely candidates
They generally don't keep big databases of candidates on file; they use their industry contacts and their own research to identify possible candidates for the particular role they are trying to fill. It follows that the best way to get yourself noticed by a headhunter is to be well-known and respected within your industry sector. Networking and other ways of raising your profile (writing articles, giving talks, becoming known as an expert in a particular area) are therefore the best ways of increasing your chances of getting a headhunter to come looking for you.

Target a few recruitment consultancies specific to your industry sector
Word-of-mouth recommendations are useful here, or call a few consultants and ask for more information on the kinds of roles and the sectors for which they normally recruit. There's no point at all in being on the books of the wrong type of agency. Once you've identified a couple of suitable agencies, ask for a meeting. (Don't register with more than two or three agencies, by the way; you don't want three copies of your CV to be put forward for one vacancy – it smacks of desperation).

Be very clear about what you are looking for and what you have to offer
Try to build up a rapport with the consultant; because they know their market well, they will be able to give you useful advice, for example, on your CV or your market worth. As with your networking strategy, think about whether there are ways in which you can be useful to the consultant: passing on snippets of information about your industry, for example (obviously, don't give away any company secrets!).

Don't be a pest
Remember that recruitment consultants are busy people. One once described her working day to me as 'running around with my hair on fire'! Don't ruin the initial rapport you have built up by phoning them every two days to check whether they've got anything for you. A quick update phone call once a fortnight is more than sufficient.

Be available
If a vacancy does arise that a consultant thinks might be suitable for you, they won't wait around for days for you to call them back. Things move quickly in the

recruitment industry and you need to be able to respond to that, and to be prepared to go for interviews at short notice.

Perhaps the most effective approach of all: offer your time for free

I've deliberately left this option until last as, although it can be very effective, not every job-seeker is in a position to do this. Maybe you're still in your current role, or perhaps financially it just isn't an option. However, there are circumstances in which this could be a viable approach: if you're a recent graduate who still hasn't landed that first job, for example, or if you've been made redundant, or have a substantial financial buffer that means you can afford to leave your current job. There are a number of ways in which you can use your time to give you a real head-start in getting the kind of job you want. (These approaches are especially valuable if you are looking to change both your role and your industry at the same time, or if you have relatively little work experience.) They may seem time-consuming, demanding and even expensive (in terms of your needing to take time out from work, for example), but remember that a career change is a big move. You owe it to yourself to have as much information as possible to inform your decision before you take the plunge.

Work-shadow

This is when you persuade someone in the role that interests you to let you shadow them for a week or two. Not only will you get an understanding of what the job involves on a daily basis (which might even put you off!), but you have the opportunity to gain a real insight into the company or organisation, as well as the wider industry. Work-shadowing can also give you some great networking opportunities.

Volunteer

Similarly, depending on the industry you're looking to move into, volunteering can be a great way of finding out more about the job, as well as making sure you're in the right place if job opportunities come up. Volunteering isn't an option only for those who are considering a move into the charitable sector, either; all sorts of organisations have opportunities for people to get involved on a voluntary basis. For example, if you're thinking about a move into marketing or event management, you could volunteer to help out with the administration of a marketing campaign, or offer to be an extra pair of hands at an event. The best way to set up opportunities like this is often via a friend or contact within the industry. The secret is to be imaginative, flexible and willing to turn your hand to anything, however mundane. One of my clients used this technique to great effect: he wrote to a well-known online travel company offering his services for free for a three-month period, and impressed them so much in that time that he was offered a full-time position on their strategy team!

Try an internship

This is really just a slightly more formalised version of volunteering. Most large companies offer internships; often they are unpaid, but you might get a daily subsistence payment. Some companies pay a small wage, and an internship is a great way of finding out whether the company is right for you, and can often be a stepping stone to a full-time paid position. Check out the websites of companies that interest you. If they don't advertise internships, consider a speculative application or use whatever contacts you have to get your CV in front of the right person.

The benefit of all of these approaches is that they give you a much better chance of being remembered if a vacancy arises in the future. Having hands-on experience will also make your CV more relevant and attractive to other prospective employers.

By now you should have a good idea of the job-search methods that are most likely to work for you, and the proportion of your search time that you should be devoting to each of these, to maximise the chances of getting the role you want. The next chapter shows you how to put together a great CV and covering letter so that, whatever job-search method you are using, you have the edge over the competition.

Chapter 12

CVs and Covering Letters

Regardless of the job-search strategies and tactics that you adopt, one thing that you must have is a stunning CV. It's one of your key job-hunting tools and it's well worth investing time and effort in writing it.

The starting point for writing a CV that will achieve things for you is to be clear about exactly what a CV is for. Your CV is, fundamentally, a marketing tool; it's your sales brochure, if you like, or your 'trailer'. It's the document that recruiters and potential employers will use to decide whether you're worth an interview. A CV will not, on its own, get you the job you want. What it should do, however, is help to get you the opportunity to interview for the job. (I say 'help' because, depending on the job-search strategy that you are adopting in any particular situation, the role of your CV will vary slightly. If you are responding to an advertisement, for example, the CV will probably be the first information about you that the recruiter receives; if your application is in response to a networking conversation, however, your CV will be more of a follow-up document. Either way, it needs to be tip-top.)

The quality of your CV will depend on its **content** and its **presentation**. Both are equally important in their own way; many suitable candidates have undoubtedly had their CVs chucked in the bin because they were too hard to read; at the same time, slick presentation won't make up for a lack of substance. Here, then, are some key points on content and presentation.

Content

Think from the recruiter's perspective

What will the job really involve. and what are the recruiters looking for in a candidate? To answer this question, you'll need to do some research (if you're following the rule of only applying for jobs in industries and companies that really interest you, you should know much of this already!). Where is the company or organisation placed within its industry? Who are its main competitors or partners? What challenges is the company – and the industry as a whole – facing or likely to face? What have been the company's recent successes, as well as less impressive aspects of its performance? Much of this information will be available on the company's website or in its annual reports. Of course, you don't expect businesses to publicise their problems, and this is where a bit of judicious analysis of third-party comment comes in: what have other people been saying about the organisation? Read the business pages of the broadsheet newspapers and relevant trade publications; www.ft.com is a good source of informed commentary. Don't be tempted to skip this stage. Not only can it make all the difference to the success of your CV; it will also provide critical information for the interview process.

Think about exactly what this specific job is likely to involve
A good question to ask yourself is: 'What problem/problems does the employer want the post-holder to solve?' Organisations don't recruit for the fun of it: they won't spend money on recruiting for and filling a position unless that post is critical to the success of the company. This rule applies just as much to more junior positions as to senior management roles, by the way. So you need to push the recruiter's buttons by demonstrating that you understand their business, the role you're applying for in the context of that business, and that you have the key attributes required for success in the role. Think about what those key attributes are. Even if the job description includes a person specification, some of the skills listed will be more important than others, and it's your task to identify which those are and tailor your CV accordingly. At this stage, double-check that the key skills required are a close match to your own analysis of your skills, strengths and style (Chapter 3). If they don't match up well, then it's probably not the job for you.

Use your achievements to demonstrate that you have the attributes the job requires
Where possible, quantify what you say: how many new customers did you bring in? By how much did you exceed sales targets? Try to give concrete evidence of your successes, and not just subjective descriptions of your ability. At this stage, think also about the specifics of your own situation with respect to this role; for example, if it would be a promotion for you, you need to demonstrate that you're ready to take on more responsibility; if it would be a change of direction for you, on the other hand, then you need to emphasise your transferable skills and your understanding of what the role involves.

Interests and leisure pursuits
Include these only if they are actually interesting! It's a waste of space to write 'reading, socialising and going to the gym'. Equally, don't include anything too quirky or far out: not everyone would feel comfortable about the idea of working with a white witch.

Tailor your CV for every application you make
The basis of it will remain the same, of course, but you will need to tweak it for each different opportunity so that you are emphasising the most relevant points.

If this sounds like a lot of effort, remember that it's much more effective to send out a few carefully targeted and prepared applications than to make lots of applications but spend very little time on each one. Recruiters can spot a generic or hastily-constructed CV a mile away.

Presentation

Write it yourself
There are plenty of companies out there that will take your hard-earned cash (often hundreds of pounds) to write your CV for you. In my opinion, they're doing you no favours. The whole point about your CV is that it is meant to tell the employer something about *you*: your style, your priorities, your personality. A professionally-written CV is unlikely to do that.

Make it easy to read
Having said that, while you want your CV to express your personality and talents, you need to follow standard presentation practice so that you reduce the risk of being eliminated because the recruiter doesn't make the effort to read your CV properly. The golden rule is to keep it clear. You should be aiming for no more than two sides of text, in an easy-to-read font and font size (Times New Roman or Arial size 12 are good). Avoid dense blocks of text by using bullet points and judicious use of bold or underlining. Avoid italics, which are hard on the eye.

Make an impact
The average length of time that the recipient of your CV will spend reading it will probably be somewhere between 10 and 30 seconds, so you need to make an immediate impact. That means that you need to have caught their eye and imagination by the time they have scanned halfway down the first page.

Get the basics right
Start with your name and brief personal details at the top of the page. (Don't top the page with the words 'Curriculum Vitae'; of course it's your CV, what else would it be?). Include your address, phone number and email address, but not your date of birth, marital status or the fact that you have 2.4 children. Make sure your email address is a credible one; sexybabe@hotmail.com might be fine for your friends, but not for job applications! Equally, don't use your current work email address: a prospective employer won't like to see you playing fast and loose with another company's time and resources.

Construct your profile
Now write your personal profile. This should be a concise, focused list of your five or six key attributes and achievements, set out in bullet points. Not every

recruiter or career expert loves this approach, but you can't please everyone, and most people find that it makes it easier to get a quick picture of the candidate. A word of warning: don't write a list of unsubstantiated adjectives. You need to give evidence of what you have to offer. Think about what makes you special, and use interesting words and compelling facts to demonstrate it.

Next, list your work experience and achievements

Again, career consultants argue about whether these should be listed in chronological or some other order (for example, according to functional areas in which you have experience). The latter approach can work if you have gaps in your career history, or if you have moved jobs or careers a number of times already. Personally, I prefer the reverse chronological approach (i.e., most recent job first); in my experience, it's the easiest to read and understand. If some of your most relevant experience is not from your current or most recent job, you can always flag it up in your personal profile.

Write in note form

A CV littered with endless sentences starting with 'I' is nauseating to read. The third person ('John Smith is an experienced marketing manager in the FMCG sector who has consistently exceeded his sales targets') is stuffy and long-winded. Cut out the pronouns and concentrate on verbs without their subjects: 'Marketing manager with extensive experience of FMCG sector and 100 per cent record in exceeding sales targets' tells you more in fewer words.

Check, check, check

When faced with hundreds of applications for one job, recruiters will use any excuse to put your CV in the 'no' pile. When sifting applications, I've been known to bin a CV on the basis of one typo: not just because I'm a pedant by nature, but because hundreds of equally well-qualified graduates had applied for a very few posts, and I had to find some way of differentiating between them. Don't give anyone the chance to do the same to you. And by the way, don't depend on spell-check programmes: not only are most of them based on US spelling, but they can't determine the sense of what you write. So if, for example, you used 'principle' when you should have used 'principal', the spell-checker won't pick it up.

Delivering your CV

If you're posting or hand-delivering a hard copy of your CV, follow these rules.
- Use good-quality, plain white paper.
- Use a high-quality printer and print out individual copies rather than photocopying them.
- Attach your covering letter (see below) to the CV - it's easy for them to get separated.

- Use a good-quality A4 envelope, so that the document doesn't get bent or folded.
- Write the name and address of the recipient neatly and clearly: first impressions count.
- If you're posting your CV, use a first-class stamp. You don't want to send the message that you think the opportunity is second-class.
- Wherever possible, avoid faxing a CV: the print-out is likely to be fuzzy and on poor quality paper, and will do you no favours.

Having said all of this, however, most job advertisements and recruitment agencies these days ask for CVs and covering letters to be sent by email. Again, rules of etiquette apply.

- Send your CV as a Word attachment. Put the same amount of care into writing it as you would into one that you would post or deliver by hand; just because you can send it off at the click of a button doesn't mean that you should spend less time on it.
- Your covering email should act as your covering letter (see next section for more advice on covering letters). Err on the side of formality: just because it's an email doesn't mean that it's not important. It's the first impression you will create. Your message needs to be polite and concise, and needs to get across the key points about your application. Don't even think about using smilies or other casual email techniques. I once had an applicant sign off an email application with 'xx', and I would *not* recommend it!
- Don't forget to attach your CV to the email. We've all done it - sent an email without its attachment and then had to re-send it with an apologetic message. Not a good look.

Finally, some companies (and many online recruitment sites) will have their own pro forma or application form for you to fill in instead of a traditional CV. If so, the same general rules apply: keep your application concise and focused, and take the time you need properly to tailor the information about yourself to the requirements of the job. Don't think that you can get away with dashing something off on the off-chance; you can't, and you're wasting your time if you do.

Covering letters

In most situations, your CV is only one-half of the application; the other part is the covering letter that accompanies it. In many cases, this is even more important than the CV because it is what the recruiter will read first. If you don't engage them with your letter, they're probably not even going to bother looking at your CV. Moreover, a covering letter gives you an opportunity to let a bit more of your personality shine through.

Broadly, there are two situations in which you will need a covering letter:

where you are replying to a job advertisement, and where you are making a speculative application. There are some rules that apply to both.

- Personalise the letter. Find out the name of the person to whom you should be addressing it. If that information is not included in the advertisement (or it's a speculative application), call the HR department or check out the company's website. However, don't use their first name, even if you've been given it: most people prefer to be addressed by their title when they're being contacted by a complete stranger. If the addressee is female, try to find out their preferred form of address (Miss/Mrs/Ms); getting this wrong can be disproportionately irritating to the recipient, and can even result in your letter getting binned (I should know, I've done it!). Similarly, *always* make sure you spell their name correctly.
- Aim for a maximum of three paragraphs, in which you need to get across why you're interested in the position (or, in the case of a speculative application, the company); how you meet the requirements of the post (or, for a speculative application, what you can bring to the company); and the outcome you are seeking (an interview or – probably more appropriate and less pushy for a speculative approach – a meeting).
- Your opening sentence needs to be eye-catching. If you're responding to an advertisement, say why the job caught your eye: *don't* write simply 'I am responding to the advertisement for the post of'. If your application is speculative, this is even more important; make sure you have a hook with which to open your letter. For example, you might have read in the national press that the company is looking to expand in an area where you have expertise. Making use of this information to introduce yourself shows that you are alert to the industry and have taken an interest in the company, which will get you off on the right footing.
- Keep your style short and punchy; avoid cumbersome words and long sentences. Your style should be more conversational than your CV, but not too informal. Try to get across a real sense of your interest in and enthusiasm for the job/company. Use bullet points to break up the text and draw attention to the key points you want to make.
- Be very clear about what those points are. Again, try to think from the perspective of the person reading the letter. If you are responding to an advertisement, make sure your letter highlights the three or four key attributes and experiences that make you perfect for the job. Consult the job description and specification, but don't just copy out its key phrases. If your application is speculative, you'll need to think about this a bit more deeply. Ask yourself which of your skills and achievements are most likely to be relevant and useful to the company and concentrate on those.
- Conclude the letter with a request for action: if you're replying to a job advertisement, it's enough to say that you look forward to hearing from the

recipient shortly. If your application is speculative, it's better to be more specific; for example, say that you would welcome the opportunity to have a chat about possible opportunities.

● The same presentational rules apply as for CVs: clear presentation, good quality paper and printing. And don't forget to sign the letter!

If you follow this guidance, you will be giving yourself the best possible chance of getting to the critical stage: interview. The following chapters take you through how to prepare for, and excel at, the interview stage.

Chapter 13

Excelling at Interview

If you persist with the approach to job-hunting that this book sets out, sooner or later (sooner, with any luck!) your efforts will pay off and you will be invited to interview. This is where the hard work really starts. Whether it's a formal interview for a job that has been advertised, or a less formal chat that you have managed to arrange by networking, the same key rule applies: prepare, prepare, prepare. The interview is the one opportunity you have to make a good impression, and you need to make it count.

Interview preparation

- Find out in advance the name(s) of the person or people who are going to be interviewing you, and as much about them as you can: their career history, how long they've been with the company, their areas of interest and expertise. The company website and annual report might contain some of this information; otherwise, try a Google search. If you can find a photograph of them, so much the better. Having an idea of what your interviewer looks like can help you to prepare mentally.

- Also find out as much as you can about the format of the interview. Will it be a traditional interview situation, or will you be expected to give a presentation or take other forms of tests (see below)? If the letter inviting you to interview doesn't contain this information, don't hesitate to call and ask; it's all a crucial part of your preparation.

- There's no such thing as too much preparation. However, you need to spend your preparation time as productively as possible. The best way to do this is to think about things from the interviewer's perspective. What do they want to find out about you? Basically, they want to know three things: can you do the job, do you really want the job, and will you fit into the organisation? They need to know this because, if you can't do the job, or if you decide you don't want it after all, or if you don't fit in with the company, they are going to find themselves advertising for your replacement in a very short time.

- Can you do the job? To demonstrate that you can, you need to be as clear as you can about what the job will actually entail, and show how your skills and experience make you the perfect match. Go through the job description/person specification with a fine toothcomb and make sure that you can offer specific, quantified examples of your achievements and experience that are relevant to what the role will demand. Remember that employers don't recruit new staff for the sake of it, so the key question to ask yourself is: 'What is the problem that they want the post-holder to solve?' You need to understand the nature of the business, the challenges likely to be facing the company and the industry more generally, and what your priorities in the role would be. In fact, it's a good idea to write a mini-business plan in advance of your interview. Set out what you see as the priorities of the role, and how you would tackle them in your first week/month/three months in the job. You're going to be asked about this at interview, in one way or another, so make sure you've given it plenty of thought. Clearly, if your interview is a speculative one, and there is no specific job on the table, you're going to have to approach this slightly differently. However, the key questions to ask are still: 'What is the problem that I could solve?' and 'How could I add value to their business?' A final point: make sure that you understand, and are comfortable with using, the appropriate business jargon. You are trying to demonstrate that you understand the industry and would fit in quickly, so it's important to be able to talk the same language as the interviewer.

- As well as your skills and experience, interviewers will be trying to identify your strengths and attributes. How do you approach things? What is your working style? Research has shown that the skills and attributes most commonly looked for are: good communication, determination, creativity, flexibility and the ability to think ahead. Make sure that you can demonstrate each of these and seek out opportunities to do so. Also think about your unique selling proposition (USP). What makes you different? What can you bring to the job that others can't? What's your X-factor?

- Do you want the job? This is where you need to demonstrate not only that you understand what the role entails, but why you want it and how you see it fitting into your longer-term career planning. You need to be able to describe why the industry interests you, and why you have chosen to apply to this particular company or organisation rather than one of its competitors. What do you see as the benefits for you of working for this particular employer? For example, you might be attracted by its reputation as the best in the field, by its client list and the business areas in which it specialises, or by the opportunities it offers for professional advancement or working abroad. Show that you have an understanding of what differentiates it from other employers in the field, and be able to explain why that is attractive to you.

- Will you fit in? This is where you need to show that you share the company's values and ethos. For example, if the company encourages its staff to work autonomously, or to take on responsibility, or to contribute new ideas to the business, you need to show respectively that you are able to work on your own initiative, keen to assume responsibility, or a creative thinker. The company website and other promotional material will tell you a lot about what the company values; be sure to read between the lines, too. And make use of business commentaries and the relevant trade press to get further clues about what the organisation *really* regards as its priorities, and how success is measured. Even better, think about who you know – or whom someone else might know – who has worked for the company or organisation. They'll be able to give you an invaluable insight to what it's like on the ground, on a day-to-day basis. You also need to be able to talk in an articulate way about your own values: what motivates you, what your preferred working style is, what your personal strengths are. Make sure that you can relate these to the organisation's own needs and values.

If you can answer these three questions, and give interesting and concrete examples to back up your answers, you will be pretty well prepared.

Practical tips

As well as all the research and preparation you need to do in advance of the interview, there is a range of practical things you can do to help ensure that you give of your best on the day.

- Make sure you know where you are going! If at all possible, do a practice run of your journey so that you know exactly where you have to get to, your route and how long it will take. Allow plenty of time: the last thing you want is to turn up late, or stressed because you thought you were going to be late.
- Dress appropriately. Below, Sue Cocks of QC Image Consultancy (www.qcimageconsultancy.co.uk) gives her top tips for dressing for interview.

Interview Do's and Don'ts

1   Do not wear a black suit; navy or grey is best.
2   Do not wear a white shirt; it implies that you are boring and unimaginative. Add colour for impact; purple, pink and green are good combinations with sober suits.
3   Guys: do not wear more than two patterns. If you are wearing a pinstripe suit, keep the shirt plain.
4   Accessorising completes the look, but do not be tempted to go over the top. Keep jewellery to a minimum.
5   Never, ever take a cheap biro with you; producing a quality pen speaks volumes.
6   Ladies: always wear tights, even if it's 110 degrees, and have a spare pair in your handbag.
7   Guys: your socks must match your trousers and must be plain; jokey socks will cost you the job.
8   Guys: do not fill your pockets with your personal paraphernalia. Invest in a briefcase; there are some very trendy cases out there. Ladies: invest in a good-quality leather handbag.
9   Polish your shoes and get them heeled if they need it. One of the first things people notice is the state of your shoes.

10 Get your hair cut; if you have long hair, ladies, put it up in a trendy style. Do not just pin it up without much thought.

11 Ladies: make-up should be worn at all times, unless you are happy to earn 25 per cent less than your peers.

12 Guys: make sure you shave, unless you are happy to earn 25 per cent less than your peers.

13 Check your appearance in a full-length mirror before you leave your home.

14 Never, ever wear an item of clothing that is stained or needs repair; people will notice and remember you for it.

- Remember that you are on display from the minute you enter the building. The interviewer could well ask the receptionist or other people that you meet for their first impressions of you, so be polite and courteous with everyone you encounter. This should go without saying, of course, but you'd be surprised how many people let themselves down by thinking that it's only the interview itself that matters.

- First impressions count: rightly or wrongly, someone will make an initial judgement about you within the first 90 seconds or so of meeting you. If the initial impression you make is poor, it will be difficult to change that during the rest of the interview, so make sure you impress from the start. When you are introduced to your interviewer(s), make eye contact, smile and shake hands firmly. Be ready to make a little small talk if they are escorting you to the interview room: don't prattle on, but avoid a stony silence. If you are offered tea or coffee, it's generally best to decline, although it's fine to request a glass of water if there isn't one already on the table.

- Try to relax. This is much more easily said than done of course! But remember that it's perfectly natural to be nervous. In any case, you'll find that a bit of adrenalin will help to keep you sharp. A good interviewer will be keen to see you at your best, so they will probably try to help you compose yourself, perhaps by asking you a couple of ice-breaker questions about your journey, for example.

- Be aware of your voice and body language. Your body language and tone of voice make up about 65 per cent of the message that you convey; words account for only 35 per cent. Make sure that you are sitting upright, and that your gestures are open; don't cross your arms or legs, and don't fidget with your hair, your jewellery or anything else. Maintain regular eye contact, but don't stare constantly at your interviewer either. If you are being interviewed by more than one person, address your response to the person who asks the question, but make sure that you use eye contact to include the other members of the panel in your conversation. Smile and be enthusiastic (but not gushing); you really want this job, remember, so you need to get your enthusiasm across. Avoid talking in a monotone; vary the speed and tone of your voice as you would in normal conversation. Be aware of your verbal tics ('sort of', 'you know', 'um...')

and make a real effort to eliminate them from your speech. (Taping yourself and listening back is a good way of identifying these.) Please don't raise your voice at the end of a sentence, as if you were asking a question; not only does it imply a lack of confidence, but it's also extremely grating for the listener!

- Once the interview gets under way, try to stay focused on the main points that you want to get across. Remember that the interviewer is trying to find out whether you are a good fit: can you do the job, do you want it and are you the right sort of person for the organisation? If you've prepared thoroughly, you should be able to demonstrate that you are indeed suitable. Answer the questions you are asked as fully as you can, but don't waffle. You need to keep the interviewer's attention at all times, so don't ramble on until they get distracted.

- Concentrate on using positive terminology. For example, avoid terms like 'problem'; say 'challenge' instead. This is especially important if you are asked about why you want to leave your current job (which you almost certainly will be). Avoid being critical of your current employer; instead, phrase your answer positively in terms of your personal and career development, and your desire to progress and make a contribution in a new environment.

- At the end of the interview, you will probably be asked if you have any questions. On no account say 'no'! Nor is this the time to ask about issues like pay, holidays or working hours. Instead, be ready to ask a couple of questions that further demonstrate your interest in the company and the research you have done. For example, you might have noticed in the company's annual report that they are planning to expand a particular area of their business. You could refer to that, or you could show your wider knowledge of the industry by asking about the implications for the business of new government regulations. Another tactic is to ask a question that demonstrates your enthusiasm or willingness to learn; for instance, you could enquire about the opportunities for learning about other areas of the business, or undertaking a professional qualification. Also, remember that an interview is a two-way process: just as the interviewer is trying to work out how good a fit you are for the job, you are trying to find out about your potential employer to see whether it is a good match for you. So if you have questions about the nature of the work, or the culture of the company, ask them. Limit yourself to one or two key questions, however; don't give the interviewer a grilling!

- If, at the end of the interview, you still really want the job (and you might not: remember what I said about this being a two-way process), don't be afraid to make that clear. Tell the interviewer that you've enjoyed your conversation, that you're even more convinced than you were before that you would be a good fit with the organisation, and that you'd really like the opportunity to show what you can deliver. It's a good way of ending the interview on a positive, upbeat note.

- Some career consultants suggest following up the interview with a letter thanking the interviewer for their time and re-stating your interest in the position on offer. Frankly, I don't recommend this; it just looks as if you are trying a bit *too* hard. In any case, it's unlikely to affect the interviewer's judgement: the chances are they will have made up their mind before your letter arrives on their desk.

Difficult interview situations

Of course, not every interview will follow the smooth pattern implied in the advice above. You might find yourself faced with an interviewer who is aggressive, distracted or who won't let you get a word in edgewise (yes, it happens). Not everyone who finds themselves having to interview prospective employees has been trained in effective interview techniques. However, regardless of the shortcomings of the person on the other side of the table, you still need to find a way to impress. Here are my tips on how to handle some of the more common tricky situations that can arise.

- An aggressive interviewer. 'Stress' interviews are probably less common than they used to be, but you could still find yourself in a situation in which the interviewer is aggressive or abrupt. The key is to keep your cool; don't rise to the bait, whether it is intentional or not. Stay clam and courteous and don't let yourself get flustered.
- An interviewer who talks too much. This is a classic symptom of an inexperienced interviewer. Sometimes, however, an interviewer will use this technique deliberately to see how assertive you are, so don't just sit there passively while they prattle on. Your best bet in this situation is to listen carefully, nodding agreement with what they are saying, and find an opportunity to come in on the back of a comment they have made.
- Being asked an inappropriate question. Most employers are well aware of the risks of asking inappropriate questions at interview: for example, whether you're planning to have a family, or questions about your political beliefs (unless, of course, these are relevant to the job, which they would be if you were being interviewed for a role as an MP's researcher, for example). But it still happens. The best response is to say that you are happy to answer the question, although you are not sure that it is very relevant. This gives the interviewer an opportunity to backtrack if they realise that they have overstepped the mark. On no account should you respond in a way that makes the interviewer look awkward or feel embarrassed; that will do you no favours at all, even if you are in the right and they are in the wrong.
- Being asked to give a presentation that you weren't forewarned about. Whatever unexpected turn the interview takes, you need to maintain your composure. If you have prepared thoroughly, you should be able to handle whatever task or challenge is thrown at you. Take a little time to gather

your thoughts, and remember the key points that you want to get across. Every other candidate is likely to be subjected to the same experience, and one of the key things that the interviewer will be looking for is your ability to handle pressure and a situation you weren't expecting. So stay calm and do your best.

- Being asked quirky questions. As I've said already, you need to be able to talk about yourself and your experiences in an interesting and compelling way. Some interviewers will go a bit further, however, and ask questions that they imagine you won't be expecting. These kinds of questions broadly fall into two categories: those that, however silly they appear, require some kind of reasoned response ('How many ping pong balls could you fit into a Boeing 747?' 'How many piano tuners are there in the world?'), and those that are looking for an opinion or some information about yourself ('Who's your hero?', 'Who's your least favourite member of the Shadow Cabinet and why?') The best approach to the first kind of question is to think about what information you would need to have to answer the question (What's the world's population? What proportion of them are likely to have a piano? How many pianos can a piano tuner tune in one day?), and base your answer on reasonable 'best guess' assumptions about the answers to those questions. The interviewer is trying to test your reasoning ability (or they might just be having a bit of fun!). Either way, think as logically as you can and explain the assumptions you make in reaching your answer. For the second type of question, the best approach is to try to relate your answer to the company in some way. So, for example, if you are being interviewed for a job with a firm of lawyers and are asked who your hero is, pick someone who has some connection with the legal field. Don't, however, spend lots of time trying to anticipate this kind of question: your preparation time is far better spent making sure that you are able to talk in an informed way about the business, the industry and how your skills and experience match the job on offer.
- An interviewer who is constantly interrupted. This really shouldn't happen, but if your interviewer is interrupted or appears distracted, he or she is not going to be giving you their full attention. In this situation, it's perfectly reasonable to ask to stop the interview temporarily, or even to re-schedule. Just be careful how you phrase your request; you want to give the impression that you are trying to be considerate of, and helpful to, the interviewer, not that you are irritated by the situation.

Alternative or additional types of interview

Many organisations will complement the traditional type of interview described above with some or all of a range of other tests and exercises. It is likely that you will be told in advance if you have to undertake such tests. Here are the most common ones, and how to prepare for and handle them.

Telephone interviews

Particularly if the initial sift for the post is being undertaken by a recruitment consultant, you might well have to undertake a telephone interview. Pretty much the same rules apply as for a face-to-face interview: be prepared, be polite and be focused. If the call comes at an inconvenient time, it's perfectly acceptable to ask if you can call back, but try to make sure it's on the same day if at all possible, or the interviewer might simply decide to give you a miss. Your tone of voice is especially important in a telephone interview, as the interviewer can't read your body language. Keep it upbeat, but don't speak too fast. Don't be tempted to fill a silence at the other end of the phone; make the point you want to make and then wait for the interviewer to respond.

Personality or psychometric tests

These are intended to identify things like your motivations and your working style. The best approach is simply to answer the questions as honestly as you can. If you try to identify the 'correct' answers, you're likely to end up tripping yourself up and being inconsistent. And, in any case, if your answers don't correspond with what the organisation is looking for, the job is unlikely to be the right one for you.

Aptitude or skills tests

These are designed to test particular aspects of your abilities: for example, numeracy or verbal reasoning. For this kind of test, you can improve your performance by practice. The company might well send you a practice sheet in advance of your interview, and there are plenty of books and websites that offer sample tests.

Written exercises

These can take a variety of forms, but the most common are 'in-tray' exercises (in which you have to make decisions about the relative priority of different tasks and indicate how you would handle them) and analysis or case study exercises (in which you are given a large amount of information and asked to recommend options for action). The exercises may or may not be relevant to the subject matter of the role for which you are applying. The keys to handling these kinds of exercise are as follows.

- Plan your time properly; in particular, make sure you leave enough time for writing up your conclusions or recommendations.
- Try to put yourself in the position of your employer: based on your research into the company, what would they be likely to regard as priorities or best options?
- Be as logical as you can, and make sure that you explain the rationale for the decisions you make or options you choose. Often there will be no 'right' answer

- the company wants to see how well you think under pressure.

Group exercises

Common at assessment centres, group exercises can strike panic into even the most seasoned interviewee. But there should be no need to panic if you remember these basic points.

- Make sure you are clear at the outset about what is required from you as a group and as individuals. If you are not clear about anything, ask! Far better to risk appearing a little uncertain than to look foolish when you take the group down completely the wrong track because you misunderstood what you were being asked to do.
- The purpose of a group exercise is – not surprisingly – to see how you perform in a team environment. You would be amazed how many people don't realise this, or forget it in the heat of the moment. Focus on demonstrating your leadership and communication skills, as well as your flexibility and creativity. Look for a win–win situation if at all possible, rather than trying to compete with the other group members. Be collaborative, not combative.
- Making an impact is not about speaking the most or the loudest. Yes, you must make a real contribution to the task (assessors can't reach a positive view about you if you don't say anything!), but take care not to dominate the discussion, and to draw in others, particularly anyone who is reticent or seems overwhelmed by the situation.
- Finally, don't try to role-play and be someone you're not. You won't be able to sustain it throughout the exercise and, in any case, as I've said before, you don't want to end up being offered a job that doesn't play to your natural working approach. Of course you want to portray yourself in your best light, but don't try to be someone that you simply aren't.

In all of the above situations, the critical point is to be clear about what is expected of you, including how much time you have. Monitor your time carefully; often it is more important to complete the exercises than to get every question absolutely correct or to come up with the 'right' answer.

Finally, you might be asked along to a 'social' interview, usually as the final part of the recruitment process. This normally involves meeting some combination of your potential colleagues, team or managers, and is another opportunity for people in the organisation to see how well you fit in. Don't be fooled: it's an interview, not a party, so make sure you behave accordingly. It's perfectly acceptable to have a glass of wine (one!) if one is offered, but I would recommend that you take your steer from others, if possible; you don't want to be the only one not on the orange juice! That said, although it's an interview, remember that the key thing people are trying to assess is whether they would like to be working with you, so do be friendly and approachable, and take an interest in other people and their roles in the organisation, without interrogating them.

If you've done your preparation properly, you should be well placed to cope with any or all of the above situations, and you'll have given yourself the best possible chance of success. The next chapter focuses on how to negotiate the best deal for yourself once you have been offered the job.

One final point: if you don't get offered the job, it's tempting to call and ask for feedback (and traditional wisdom dictates that you should). I have my doubts about how effective this is. There's a high chance that the interviewer will be too embarrassed to tell you the real reason why you were unsuccessful, and will fall back on the old line, 'another candidate fitted our requirements better'. Which is undoubtedly true, but not particularly useful. That said, if you've succeeded in landing a number of interviews but haven't been successful in any of them, it could be worth seeing if you can get an honest assessment of your performance: if not from the interviewer direct, then via a recruitment consultant if one was involved. The most important feedback is probably that which you can give yourself: what areas hadn't you prepared well enough? Did you let yourself down in any other way? What would you do differently if you were facing the interview again? Honestly answering these questions is the best way to help yourself prepare for next time.

Chapter 14

Closing the Deal

You've been offered the job. Congratulations! But before you rush to accept, you owe it to yourself to take stock one more time. However desperate you are to leave your current job, or to get back to work if you haven't been working for a while, you need to make sure that this really is the right opportunity for you. Too many people base their decisions about whether to accept a job offer on the single criterion of salary. And of course remuneration – which encompasses much more than just your basic pay, as we'll see below – is an important issue. But it's not the first thing that you should consider when you're trying to make your mind up. Here are the other questions you need to ask yourself, and try to answer honestly.

Do I have all the information I need to make this decision?

Your research and preparation for interview will have given you a good overview of the organisation, but it's unlikely to have uncovered everything that you need to know. Equally, the interview itself is likely to have thrown up new areas that you need to think about, and although you might have got the answers to some of your questions during the course of the interview, you'll probably have other queries that you didn't get the opportunity to raise at the time. Issues that you really need to be clear about include the following.

Why is there a vacancy?

This may well have been covered at interview, but if the previous incumbent left the role under a cloud, for whatever reason, this might be something that the interviewer skirted over and that you didn't feel comfortable enough to ask about. Now is the time to clarify this. You need to know if you will be taking on a problem department, a problem boss or just a problem! Of course, even after you have been offered the job, an employer might be reluctant to tell you the truth in case it puts you off. Use your network to help shed some light on the issue if you can. Failing that, don't be afraid to use your gut instinct. Do you sense that people are being deliberately evasive when you raise this question?

Am I clear about what the job will actually entail on a day-to-day basis?

If not, seek clarification. The interview will have focused on you and how well you fit the job description, but you need to double-check that the job description accurately reflects the job itself. Make sure that you are clear about your manager's priorities, and the tasks on which you are likely, in practice, to spend the majority of your time.

Have I met everyone who will have a key impact on my role?

Your immediate manager was probably the person – or one of the people – who interviewed you, but be clear about other people with whom you will need to work closely and/or report to, and try to get to meet them too. You don't want to find out too late that the marketing manager with whom you have day-to-day contact is an ogre who was deliberately kept out of your way during the selection process!

How will my performance be measured?

This is not just about the formal appraisal process: it's about the key results that your manager will be looking for. Are you confident that you can deliver them, and want to deliver them? What would be the consequences of not meeting your targets or objectives?

Did the interview throw up any unexpected information, or any further questions that I need to ask?

It's possible that the interviewer raised issues or areas that were not fully reflected in the job description, for example. What implications do these have for your role, how you will be spending your time, and your fit with the organisation?

What does my gut instinct tell me?

You've had an opportunity to meet your prospective manager(s), possibly even some of your colleagues and/or staff, and you've had a glimpse of the organisation itself from the inside. How do you feel about it? Do the people you meet seem like people you can get on with? Is the working environment one that will suit you? Don't ignore any alarm bells that ring: your gut instinct can be as sound a basis for a decision as anything else. If there is something about which you feel uneasy, how much is it likely to affect your day-to-day work? For example, you might find it easier to adapt to an open-plan office than to work for a manager who you sense has a very different style from yours.

Remuneration

If, having answered these questions, you still feel the role is right for you, then and only then is it time to consider the issue of remuneration. I say 'remuneration' because it's not just about your salary: you need to consider the whole benefits package on offer before you can decide whether it represents what you regard as adequate reward. There are several elements to take into account.

1 **Pay**. Is the salary in line with your expectations, based on the level of responsibility you will have, and the going market rate for this kind of role? It can be difficult to work this out, as different industries and companies will have varying rates of pay for jobs that are actually quite similar. A friendly

recruitment consultant, or a contact within the industry, might be able to shed some light on this for you.

2 **Bonus/commission**. Is there a bonus or commission system? How much could you reasonably expect this to add to your basic salary? How are bonuses or commission payments awarded, how soon would you be eligible to be part of this scheme, and how regularly are awards made? For example, will you need to have been in post for a year before a bonus would be awarded, or is performance assessed or rewarded on a more frequent basis?

3 **Pension**. What pension arrangements are in place? Is it a final-salary scheme (unlikely these days!) or some other kind? What contribution does the employer make and what are your contributions? Is there scope for you to make additional voluntary contributions, or to transfer an existing pension into the employer's scheme? Is there a qualifying period before you are eligible to join the scheme?

4 **Hours of work**. What are your contracted hours of work and – more importantly – what is the reality about the hours you will be expected to work, or will have to work to get the job done? Is there scope for you to work flexibly: for example, can you work from home, or do five days' work in four and have a day off?

5 **Holidays**. What is your holiday entitlement? Does it increase with length of service? Is there scope for you to 'buy' extra holiday, or to carry holiday entitlement over from one year to the next?

6 **Other benefits**. What other benefits does the company offer? These could be anything from subsidised healthcare or gym membership through to discounts on the company's own products or services. How valuable are these benefits to you?

7 **Notice period**. How much notice will you have to work if you decide to move on in a year or two's time? More importantly, does your contract prevent you from working in a similar field or with clients that you acquire? Are there confidentiality clauses or other restrictions that could limit your choices for your next career move?

Only when you have considered all these elements will you be in a position to decide whether the overall package on offer meets your requirements. If there are areas that you are unsure about, seek clarification. Pension and bonus arrangements in particular can have a big impact on your overall financial situation. This is also a good time to look back at your values exercise and assess the remuneration package in relation to your priorities. For example, the pay you are being offered might be slightly lower than you hoped for, but if one of your priorities is to have more time outside work, then issues like workload, hours of work and holiday entitlement may well have a bigger bearing on your decision. Don't be afraid to negotiate. Your prospective employer has invested time, money and energy in the recruitment process and, now that they have offered you the job, they have an emotional as well as a practical attachment to you; they can see you filling the post, and they will be reluctant either to have to revert to their second-choice candidate or to advertise all over again if you turn it down. So you are in quite a strong negotiating position. Of course, most of us find it embarrassing to haggle about money, but you owe it to yourself to get the best possible package. If you don't feel comfortable with this, you might be able to enlist the help of your recruitment consultant, if one was involved in the selection process; it is in their interests that you take the job, and that you get as high remuneration as possible, as that could well affect their own rate of payment.

Of course, the employer might invite you to make *them* an offer. If this happens, resist the temptation to undersell yourself. It is easier to negotiate down than up. That said, don't make a request that is clearly ludicrous: your prospective employer might well have second thoughts about your judgement! Use what you know about current market rates to inform your opening position. Your current salary is unlikely to be a very reliable benchmark, especially if you are moving role or industry, but presumably you will want to be at least as well off as you were before. Obviously, if you are making a dramatic career change you might need to accept a salary that is lower than your current one, but make sure that you are comfortable with the overall package, because otherwise dissatisfaction can set in very quickly.

Once you have agreed an offer verbally, get it in writing, especially if you have agreed terms and conditions that are different from the norm (extra holiday entitlement, for example, or early entry to the pension scheme). This isn't because your employer isn't trustworthy (I hope!); it's simply to make sure that everyone is clear about the arrangement and that there is no scope for confusion at a later date (if you have a change of manager, for example). Don't ask for a letter setting out your key terms and conditions, either; ask for a draft contract and, if they exist, a copy of the company's staff handbook or rules for employees. Only when you have all this information should you sign on the dotted line.

Finally, what do you do if, when you hand your notice in to your current employer, they respond by making a counter-offer? Depending on how attractive the offer is, you might wish to consider it. You might also wish to let your new employer know that such an offer has been made, as it could strengthen your negotiating hand further. Don't get into a protracted bargaining game, though. And be very honest with yourself: will the new deal that your current employer is offering (promotion, more pay, more flexible hours) really compensate for all the factors that led you to look for a new job in the first place? In the vast majority of cases, the answer to this is 'no'.

Once you've made the decision to accept the job, your attention will naturally turn to getting started and making a good impact. The next section of this book takes you through how to do that. One last word of advice at this stage, though: make sure you handle your exit from your current job gracefully. This is not the time to tell your manager all his or her weaknesses and failings; you should have done that (tactfully) while you were still in the job. You never know when you are going to come across them again and need their help (and, as a minimum, they are likely to be asked for a reference), so don't burn your bridges. Do your best to leave everything shipshape, and be prepared to make yourself available for a week or two in case your manager or the new post-holder has any questions. That way you leave with your reputation intact and can look forward to your new post knowing that you haven't walked away from your old one leaving loose ends for someone else to tie up.

Chapter 15

What if None of This Works?

I'm hoping that you don't have to read this chapter! But, just so that all the bases are covered, here we go. What happens if you've identified your ideal job or business, written your action or business plan, networked like crazy, followed all the other strategies in the book, and you still haven't landed that promotion/got that new job/made any money from your business? Is it time to give up?

The answer is: it depends. All the management and self-help books on the market will tell you that perseverance is key: try, try and try again. And, to a great extent, that is true. Often we are tempted to give up when perhaps we haven't really tried hard enough. Career change is hard work. It takes time and effort. It's all too easy to get despondent and give up at the first, or second, or third attempt. We live in a society that values quick fixes, and it's tempting to quit when things don't go our way.

History and self-help books are full of examples of people who succeeded not only against the odds, but after years of trying. Roger Bannister was told he'd never run a four-minute mile. Elvis Presley's teacher told him he couldn't sing (!). Thomas Edison took 9,000 attempts to create the lightbulb. Nelson Mandela spent 27 years in prison before apartheid was abolished. So perseverance is important; don't give up too soon.

But it's also vital to be realistic. There's a big difference between persistence and bloody-mindedness. If you're not making any headway whatsoever, it might be time to review not just your strategy, but also your goal. As W.C. Fields famously said: 'If at first you don't succeed, try, try and try again. Then quit. No use in being a damn fool about it.' Knowing when to cut your losses is an important skill, and one that every successful business-person or entrepreneur has had to learn.

So, how do you work out if it's time to quit? If you find yourself reading this chapter because you haven't got the outcome you wanted, ask yourself these questions, and answer them *honestly*.

- Am I absolutely clear about what I want to achieve?
- Do I really, really want it?
- Am I being realistic?
- Have I devoted enough time and effort to this? Have I done my research thoroughly, made sure that my CV is as good as it possibly can be, followed up every single contact in my network, done everything that I can to improve my profile and make an impact?

- Have I *really*?
- Do I have a history of giving up too easily, or moving on when a situation becomes too difficult? Or is it my normal tendency to plough doggedly on, even when all the evidence suggests that there is no point?
- Can I afford (emotionally and financially) to keep plugging away at this, or is it time to change tack?

Some objective advice can be really helpful at this stage. Go and see a career or business coach, or make an appointment with your mentor. They might well be able to suggest different strategies or tactics that you can try. Or they could give you a reality check; sometimes it simply won't be possible for you to get the job you really want, or your business idea just won't be a runner.

If you come to the conclusion that you should admit defeat, what should you do about it? Here are some suggestions.

- **Be really clear about why you haven't succeeded**. Again, a career coach or other adviser (an objective one, *not* your friends or family) might be able to help you deal honestly with this question. It's always hard to admit failure, but if you can identify the real reason for your lack of success, it will teach you an enormous amount.
- **Check your attitude**. How much do you really want that job? Are you thinking of giving up because, frankly, it's easier than having to keep working hard to achieve your goal? Are you giving up because you're actually scared of what it might mean if you succeeded? We can self-sabotage in lots of interesting ways!
- **Learn the lessons from your experience**. Whatever the outcome of your job search or business planning, you will have learned a huge amount: about yourself, about industry sectors, about business, about other people. Think about how you can use that information to open up opportunities.
- **Think laterally**. If you haven't succeeded (despite your *best* efforts) in landing the job you really want, consider whether there are 'shadow jobs' that might offer you nearly as much satisfaction. For example, if you've been trying but failing to cut it as a journalist, you could look at areas like public relations, public affairs or copywriting. If you've just failed your accountancy exams for the third time, you could still work as a financial adviser, a business adviser within a bank, or in one of the governmental financial bodies. The clearer you can be about exactly why your chosen route isn't working for you, the easier it will be to come up with an alternative that *could* work.

Only you can decide when it's time to try a different route. But do make sure that you have given yourself the best possible chance of succeeding before you throw the towel in. Review your strategy and action plan, get the best professional advice you can afford and think about how much you want to succeed. Then, and only then, consider different options. And remember that there are plenty of them out there.

Part 3

Making an Impact

Chapter 16

Making the Right Start

The first few weeks in a new job is one of the real crunch points in your career; it's an opportunity for you to make your mark quickly and lay the foundations for your future success. Whether you've moved to a new company or gained a promotion in your current workplace, you're going to be meeting new people and facing fresh challenges. The initial impact that you make is going to determine in large part how successful you are in your new role. You need to get it right from day one. Here's how.

- **Do your homework**. There's plenty you can do to prepare for your new role even before you start. You'll already have done lots of research into the organisation and industry when you were preparing for interview, and now's the time to build on that. Once you've signed your contract, you're likely to be able to get access to more information about the company than was available to you as an outsider, so make good use of it. Ask your new manager to let you have copies of any documents that they think it would be useful for you to read in preparation for your new role; for example, the departmental business plan, an organisation chart, procedure manuals and the staff handbook if there is one. Find out as much as you can about key people and procedures.

- **Think about your key tasks and priorities**. Again, you will have done some research on these in preparation for interview. Now you need to flesh this out. Put together a draft action plan for your first day, week and month in the job. (Note that it can only be a draft at this stage, as you might well need to adapt it to specific circumstances when you arrive. But the more prepared you are, the better.) What will your key tasks be? What are your early priorities, and what research can you do to prepare yourself to tackle them? If you can, it's a good idea to sit down with your new manager in advance of your first day so that they can brief you on their objectives and priorities. After all, your manager is the person on whom first and foremost you will need to make a good impression. Show them how keen you are to do well from the very first day, and that you understand the importance of knowing their priorities.

- **Treat your first day at work like another interview**. Remember the golden rule that first impressions count, and make your first impression a good one. The chances are that you will be introduced to a lot of (possibly senior) people on your first day, so make a real effort. Dress well, get there early and be friendly with everyone.

- **Listen and learn**. Your first few weeks in the job are likely to be busy and demanding; you'll be meeting new people and encountering new processes and ways of doing things. Take a real interest in everyone and everything you come across. It's a good idea to keep a notebook in which you can jot down the names, responsibilities and contact details of people you meet - you'll never remember them all otherwise! Take the trouble to memorise names so that you can address someone by name the next time you meet them; this is one of the most effective ways of bonding with people and getting them to look favourably on you. Take every opportunity you get in the early days to see as much of the business as you can. Make a particular point of seeking out and befriending people who are most likely to be able to help you settle in and learn quickly: receptionists, secretaries and even security guards often know a huge amount about how the organisation really works.

- **Learn the rules**. Make sure you know what is expected in terms of dress code, hours of work, lunchtimes and so on. You want to be seen to fit in quickly and you certainly don't want to step on toes by getting simple – and noticeable – things wrong in the early days. In terms of your role, make sure that you are clear about key routines and events such as reporting cycles, or the timing and format of management meetings. Be especially clear about your authority levels in relation to any staff or budget you have to manage.

- **Don't criticise**. Even if you've been brought in to the organisation to do precisely that – to turn round a failing department, for example – keep your counsel in the early days. Talk to your team, your colleagues and your manager before drawing any firm conclusions. Resist the temptation to say 'we did things better in my old company'. You will have plenty of opportunities to identify and suggest improvements as you settle into your role, so don't get off on the wrong footing. Your most important priority is to build up good relationships, so don't do anything that could jeopardise that and make people resent you.

- **Connect**. If your new colleagues invite you for a drink at the end of your first day or week, accept. Socialising with work colleagues is a great way to get to know people quickly. Moreover, one of the best ways of getting to know what's really valued in an organisation is to find out how people talk about it outside the office. Make an effort to find out the socialising pattern for your workplace: perhaps everyone goes to the pub on a Friday after work, for example. No one's saying that you have to abandon your old friends in favour of your new work colleagues, but you'll settle in much more quickly if you can build up a good rapport with the people you work with, and some socialising can really help with that.

- **Go the extra mile**. Without being a creep, make it clear from the outset that you are prepared to work hard, do more than the minimum and take on extra projects. Seeking out opportunities to get involved in different areas of the business, or to develop your role, will help you quickly to establish your reputation as a 'can-do' person, as well as give you additional early opportunities to demonstrate what you can achieve.

If you take these tips on board, you've given yourself the best possible start in your new job. The following chapters show you how to build on that, and ensure your long-term career success, by managing your attitude and actions.

Chapter 17

The Right Attitude

There are hundreds of books on the market claiming to set out the secrets of success. I reckon I've read most of them (and I've listed the ones that I think are the best in the bibliography). While each author has his or her own take on how to be successful in work and other areas of your life, there's a pretty firm consensus around a number of key attitudes and actions that seem to be practised by people who go further and faster than the rest of us.

I have already stressed the importance of having your personal definition of success, which should be about much more than just work. But, given that you've reached this stage of the book, I'm assuming that at least one element of how you define your success is in relation to your career or your business. Here then, for those of you who don't have time to read your way through the 'success' section of the bibliography, is my own summary of the attitudes (this chapter) and the actions (Chapter 18) that will help to put you in a different league. By the way, in my view these apply equally whether you are an employee or self-employed.

Take responsibility

I spend most of my time working one-to-one with clients who want to change some aspect – or every aspect! – of their careers. I know from experience that the clients who will succeed in making the changes they want are the ones who understand that they have to take responsibility for effecting those changes. Yes, as a career coach I can help my clients to identify work options to suit them, and to put together an action plan to help them get there. But I can't carry out the action plan for them. They need to be prepared to go away and put in the hours of research, networking, interview preparation or business planning. Often there are no short cuts. It takes hard work and effort, but most of all it takes an understanding that you, and only you, are responsible for your career.

People often understand this more readily if they are thinking about it in the context of setting up their own business; they know that they will have to do the planning, the marketing, the cold-calling and so on. But even if you work for a big organisation with its own HR, training and talent-management departments, you still need to grasp that the only person who is ultimately responsible for your career is you. The organisation might well have resources that you can use to help you develop – access to training, for example – but it is your responsibility and yours alone to make sure that your career path is, and continues to be, the right one for you.

Taking responsibility also means avoiding the excuses that we all come up with from time to time to explain why our lives or careers or businesses aren't the way we want them to be: 'my boss doesn't like me', 'the company doesn't care enough about its staff', 'my business isn't working because of the economic downturn'. Pretty much the worst thing you can do for your career prospects is to allow yourself to adopt a victim mentality. Not only does it make you a miserable person to be around (and see below for how badly that can affect your success), but it will drain you of energy and prevent you from taking action. Look at it this way: if you've got a complaint about something – your boss, your workplace, your job – you must have a vision of how things could be better. So do something about it. Get to know your boss better and see how you can improve your relationship; form a support group at work; talk to your manager about ways in which you can make your role more interesting or rewarding. Don't just sit there complaining and hoping that someone else will fix the problem. Take responsibility for fixing it yourself!

Of course, things will happen to us that we can't control: your post could get made redundant because of a merger, for example. You need to be able to distinguish between what you can control and what you can't. If the situation is genuinely one in which you can't exert any influence, then accept it and move on. While you can't control the situation, you can always control your *response* to that situation, and that can make all the difference. So, take our redundancy example: a victim's response would be along the lines of, 'Poor me, I always seem to be in the wrong place at the wrong time', while a person who takes responsibility will ask themselves, 'What is the opportunity for me in this situation?' Perhaps your redundancy payment will help you to launch the new business you've always wanted to try, or maybe redundancy was the kick you actually needed to re-think your career. Look for opportunities, not obstacles.

Be focused

It's well documented that people who write down their goals are more likely to achieve them than those who don't. Why? Because they have more focus. They know exactly what they're working towards, so it's easier for them to make good decisions about how they spend their time and energy.

Whether you're making strategic plans for your life or your business, or you're trying to plan a project or meeting at work, the rule is the same: you need to know what outcome you want to achieve. Only when you're clear about the result you want will you be able to put in place the appropriate action to make it happen. As the old saying goes, 'If you don't know where you're going, then any route will do.'

Whether you're running your own business or working for someone else, be really clear about what you are trying to achieve, and therefore what your work priorities are. The clearer you are about your top priorities, the easier you will find it to use your time effectively. The starting point for identifying your priorities is to know what your strategy or purpose is: Stephen Covey, the bestselling author of *Seven Habits of Highly Effective People*, refers to this as 'starting with the end in mind'. The 'end' is not just the desired outcome or result, it's also the *purpose*: why you're doing whatever it is in the first place. Make sure you understand your organisation's mission statement and strategy. If you read them and can't make head nor tail of them because they're a load of empty management-speak, talk to your boss and/or senior people in the organisation and ask them to explain what their priorities are. Your success in an organisation will depend on the extent to which you are seen to help it achieve its goals, so find out exactly what those goals are.

Chapter 18 gives you lots of tips on how to manage your time and energy so that you can do an effective job and still go home on time. But focus is as much about mindset as about action, which is why I've included it in this chapter, too. You need to be mentally prepared to be ruthless; to be 100 per cent clear about what you are trying to achieve, and to dump or delegate the stuff that isn't going to contribute to that. Think about the activities that really produce results in your work. Focus on doing those and doing them better. Remember the 80/20 rule: 80 per cent of what you achieve comes from 20 per cent of your effort. Focus on that 20 per cent and get rid of the stuff you don't need. Focus on using your signature strengths. Think about and develop your niche: which specific area of expertise do you have, or can you develop, that will really increase the contribution you make?

The point of being focused, planning and setting goals is not to become so efficient that you can pack even more stuff into your diary. In fact, it's quite the opposite: being clear about your priorities and how you are going to achieve them will free up your time and energy so that you have space to think. The less busy and consumed with urgent or irrelevant tasks you are, the more opportunity you have to think about how you can be more effective and add more value, to come up with creative ideas that will take your organisation or business forward, and to nurture relationships with other people. You'll have more time to make better judgements, and you'll feel less stressed and more in control. Not bad, wouldn't you say?

Be curious

A 2002 survey of 80 US and UK business leaders examined the range of skills and qualities associated with their success. Among the answers – many of which are covered here – was having a broad range of interests. At first sight, this might seem rather a mundane criterion, but think about it a little more. People with lots of interests have a highly-developed sense of curiosity, they're knowledgeable about a wide range of subjects, and they probably have a much bigger network than most of us. As we saw in the chapter on job-search strategies (Chapter 11), people and information are the two key elements in a successful job search, and it makes sense that they should also be key elements of a successful career.

The speed of change in today's society means that you need to keep learning in order to survive. Although I've suggested above that you should develop a niche for yourself, you also need to keep abreast of what's happening in the rest of your industry, and in society as a whole. Take any opportunities you can to learn about other aspects of your business. Also, keep up-to-date with trends, public opinion and consumer behaviour. Read widely (not just in topic areas that you are familiar with), and be open-minded and ready to challenge conventional wisdom. Take courses, spend some money on personal development, and do everything you can to increase your knowledge base. Learn about other people's experiences, either first-hand or by reading biographies and business books, and use that information to broaden your own thinking. The ability to think strategically and creatively, and the ability to understand the context you are working in, are key attributes of successful professionals. The more you increase your knowledge and understanding of the world around you, the more easily you will develop these skills.

Curiosity feeds creativity; curious people are more likely to come up with creative ideas and new ways of doing things. Exposing yourself to lots of different environments and information is a great way of improving your creative thinking and making mental connections that you might not otherwise have thought of. That's how many a successful business is born. And having a wide range of interests and knowledge simply makes you a more interesting person to be around, which in turn makes the whole business of networking much easier: people want to talk to you because you always have something interesting to say.

Know yourself

Self-awareness is one of the fundamental keys to your success. As we saw at the beginning of this book, knowing who you are, what's important to you and what your skills and strengths are is critical to finding the role or position in which you can excel. It's about being 'internally referenced': knowing what's right for you, rather than focusing on other people's expectations.

This is a good time to revisit your values and skills/strengths exercises. Be very clear about what matters to you and what motivates you. How well do your lifestyle and chosen career path match up with your real values and priorities? What's missing? Where are you letting yourself down or selling yourself short?

Be equally clear about your strengths, talents and areas of relative weakness. Look at the feedback you got from the friends and colleagues who described your top features and skills. How closely do their responses fit with your own analysis of yourself? If their responses were similar to your own, that's a good sign that you are pretty self-aware: you see yourself as others see you. If, however, there were some discrepancies, think about why that might be. Perhaps you described yourself as 'assertive', for example, but other people used stronger words like 'aggressive' or 'confrontational'. Don't be afraid to go back to them and ask for specific examples of what they meant. This might feel a little uncomfortable, but it's important feedback. Be brutally honest with yourself. Can you understand how someone else might see you in a less flattering light than you see yourself? By the way, the feedback exercise isn't intended to throw up only negative discrepancies. As we've noted, sometimes other people are better at identifying your hidden skills: the things you are so good at doing that you take them for granted. Acknowledge these, because they could be the core of your USP, or brand.

Recognise your weaknesses – or, as I prefer to express it, areas in which you are less strong. Not so that you can beat yourself up about them, but so that, as I've suggested above, you can find ways of minimising them. That might mean getting people on to your team who are detail-oriented if you are more of a big-picture person, or outsourcing some parts of your business that don't come naturally to you. Knowing which are your key strengths and abilities, and what makes you unique, will enable you to direct your energy and efforts in the most productive way. Being honest about areas in which you are less strong is in itself a sign of strength.

Challenge your beliefs

Our beliefs, and especially what we believe about ourselves, have a much bigger impact on our future and our success than events, our environment or our circumstances. You only have to think of the dozens of rags-to-riches stories about people who have come through adversity to reach dizzying heights of success to see that that is true. That's because our beliefs are the single biggest factor affecting our behaviour. If we believe that we can't do something, it generally turns into a self-fulfilling prophecy.

The problem is that often our beliefs about ourselves are flawed: either they're based on other people's judgements ('My mother always told me I was lazy', 'My teacher told me I wasn't creative'), or they're based on generalisations we draw from one specific incident (you gave a presentation that didn't go very well, so you think 'I am rubbish at public speaking'). Once a negative belief has taken root, we have a tendency to find further examples that reinforce that belief, and ignore evidence that might undermine it. So, in the public speaking example above, you reinforce your belief that you're no good at giving presentations by recalling only those instances where they haven't gone very well, and you filter out incidences where actually you performed competently. You end up with a distorted view of the situation and guess what: it becomes that self-fulfilling prophecy. Because you've convinced yourself that you're no good at speaking in public, that ends up being the case.

The same problem arises in relation to our view of the world. We unquestioningly accept as fact those opinions and beliefs that we hear stated over and over again. But what would happen if you chose to challenge other people's perspectives or the conventional wisdom? How often have you heard statements like 'Most small businesses fail', and 'It's almost impossible to get into television because it's so competitive'? Says who? Lots of small businesses succeed, and become big businesses; *someone* has to work in television, so why shouldn't it be you? Similarly, who said you weren't creative? Why should their opinion be more valid than yours? What did they mean by 'creative', anyway?

Ultimately, it's down to you what you believe about yourself and the world around you, and in turn to determine your attitudes, actions and outcomes. This isn't about arrogance or self-delusion - of course there will be things that we physically or mentally aren't capable of, but too often when we say 'I can't', what we are really saying is 'Other people think I can't and I believe them', or simply 'I choose not to'.

Don't let your beliefs about what you are or aren't capable of stop you before you even start. Often we use our beliefs as an excuse for staying in our comfort zone. If you allow yourself to believe that you're not clever enough/creative enough/organised enough to set up your own business, for example, you've given yourself the excuse not to do anything about it. But if you allowed yourself to think that you *could* be capable of coming up with a good business idea, or you could have the self-discipline to make self-employment work for you, then you might actually have to do something about it and that would be scary!

Get clear about the thinking that is holding you back: your 'limiting beliefs'. Once you have identified them, you can start to undermine them and replace them with more realistic and positive thinking. Ask yourself the following questions.

- **What beliefs do I hold that are holding me back?** ('I'm stupid/lazy/disorganised.')
- **What are my 'filters' – the beliefs that affect how I view the world?** ('Very few women succeed in business'; 'You have to be ruthless to get to the top'.)

Now ask yourself the following question.

- **What would be a more positive and productive belief?** ('I'm bright and organised'; 'There are lots of very successful women, both in boardrooms and running their own business'.)

Look for evidence to back up these new beliefs. For example, make a list of all your achievements and don't stop until you get to 50 (that's 50 achievements, not 50 years old). Draw up a list of successful women you admire: City superwoman Nicola Horlick, millionaire entrepreneur Deborah Meaden, Newsnight presenter Kirsty Wark are just some examples. Use this information to challenge your limiting beliefs about yourself and what might be possible.

Underpin your work on changing your mindset by taking regular practical action. The next chapter has lots of tips, but here's an example: if you're not comfortable speaking in public and you feel that that is holding you back from where you want to be, join a Toastmasters group or a debating club and hone your skills. Pushing yourself outside your comfort zone from time to time – but not too often – will increase your self-confidence and your belief that you can achieve more.

Challenging our own and other people's perceptions, and the conventional wisdom, isn't just an effective way of reframing our beliefs about ourselves. It's also a technique that will help you in your day-to-day work. Being aware (yes, it's self-awareness again) of how you tend to approach problems or projects, and the assumptions on which you operate, can make you much more effective in your job. Questioning the accepted wisdom, looking for different ways to do things, different angles and thinking beyond the obvious will help you to come up with better and more innovative solutions and approaches. Challenge your assumptions, and you open up a whole new range of options.

Be comfortable with risk and failure

Risk and failure are facts of life. Whatever venture you are undertaking, whether it's a work project or a new business, there are no guarantees of success. Successful people understand this and have learned to deal with it.

Successful people also understand the difference between 'rash risks' and 'responsible risks'. Chucking in your job to set up your own restaurant when you have no business plan, no capital and no relevant experience is rash; with the right business plan, the right backers and the right knowledge, you are giving yourself the best opportunity of success. But however well prepared you are, you can't be 100 per cent sure that it will work out. No one ever can, except with hindsight. There's always going to be an element of risk when you try something new, because you're making a foray into the unknown. Some degree of risk is simply part of the equation.

Being able to deal with risk is one of the skills that helps people get to the top. The higher up an organisation you go, the less stable the environment you tend to be working in. The job becomes more varied and less predictable; you have a broader range of responsibility and are probably working to longer timescales. You have bigger decisions to make, with bigger potential impacts. All of these factors increase the level of uncertainty, and therefore risk, involved in your role. Being comfortable with risk, and at the same time having the ability to spot ways of minimising it, are skills that will help you boost your career.

What if it doesn't work out and you 'fail'? You'll have heard the cliches about failure: 'there's no such thing as failure, only a learning opportunity', or 'there's no failure, only feedback'. It's easy to dismiss such thinking as life-coaching mumbo-jumbo, 'Pollyanna' thinking. But they're cliches because there's a real element of truth in them. Many of my clients who have changed direction after a career 'failure' now look back and see those experiences as some of the most useful in their lives. Perhaps it finally showed them where they were going wrong; maybe it was the push they needed to change direction completely. Whatever the situation, they realised in retrospect that it was an important part of their professional and personal development.

My own experience is a good case in point. I spent ten months as Chief of Staff to Iain Duncan Smith when he was Leader of the Conservative Party. It was a role in which I 'failed'; some people would say I failed spectacularly! And it wasn't made any easier by the fact that a lot of it was played out in the media. Eventually, I chose to walk away. I was exhausted and my confidence was shattered. I can honestly say that it was the worst time of my life. But if I hadn't gone through that difficult experience, I wouldn't be where I am now: working with other people who want to change career, and enjoying a whole new career path for myself!

The two things to remember about failure are: it's universal, and it's subjective. In other words, everybody is going to 'fail' at some point. None of us goes through life with everything turning out exactly as we intended. Even people whom we all regard as successful – Richard Branson, for example – have had their share of failure. Yet, asked about the secret of his success, Branson is famously quoted as saying 'I've just failed a lot more than most people'. Equally, what society, your parents or your friends define as 'failure' needn't be your definition. Lots of my friends in the political world thought I was mad when I announced I was going to set up my own coaching business. The response to that is, 'so what?' Remember that the fundamental rule of success is that it has to be *your* definition of success, and therefore your definition of failure.

What if your fear of failure is holding you back from making changes? We looked at this in Chapter 9 but, to recap: the best way to deal with both risk and the fear of failure is to ask yourself: 'What's the worst that could possibly happen?' Then ask yourself 'If that did happen, how would I handle it?' If you have a handling strategy for your worst-case scenario, it becomes a lot less scary. There are very few failures that you can't recover from.

Successful people recognise that risk and failure are simply part of the mix of an interesting life and career. Understand that, do the best you can to minimise the risks, have a fall-back plan in place, and then just get on with it.

Be a people person

Successful people like people. They understand that relationships are the bottom line of any business. Without good business relationships, you don't have a good business. It's been said that 80 per cent of business success is down to people, and 20 per cent down to strategy (back to that 80/20 rule again!). Whether it's possible to be statistically accurate about this or not, it's abundantly clear that successful business people are people with **charisma** and **connections**. What it boils down to is how well you relate to people, and which people you know.

What are the benefits of being well-connected? You're making yourself more visible, which means that you are likely to get promoted faster (or be able to build up your business or client base more quickly) and be able to solve problems faster, because you've got access to the wisdom and experience of many other people. The better the relationships you build, the wider your sphere of influence will become, with positive knock-on effects for your career or your business. On a very practical level, work is also a lot more fun if you are surrounded by people with whom you have built up a good relationship.

So what's the secret of charisma? It's one of those qualities that you recognise in someone as soon as you meet them, but it can be hard to put your finger on exactly what makes a person charismatic. In my opinion, it's about interested and active listening. The most charismatic person I have ever met was Rudi Giuliani, the former Mayor of New York. Although I only spoke with him for a few minutes, during that time he made me feel as though I was the only person in the room. Bill Clinton is said to have the same ability. Closer to home, Jennifer Bryant-Pearson, the MD of JBP Public Relations, the biggest and most successful PR company in south-west England, is someone who oozes charisma. She takes a passionate interest in everyone she meets, she listens and asks questions much more than she talks about herself, and every time I meet her I go away with a spring in my step. That's charisma.

Connecting with people is about more than just being a good communicator. Communication is essentially about being able to get your message across to your audience clearly and succinctly. But connection goes a step further: it's about building rapport, trust and a sense that you have something in common. Essentially, it's about empathy: being able to put yourself in someone else's shoes and see things from their perspective. It's about thinking, 'What can I give?' rather than, 'What can I get?'

We covered the practical points of networking as part of your job-search in Chapter 11, and pretty much the same rules apply to networking – or building up connections and relationships – in the workplace or when you are running your own business. The golden rule is, 'give before you take'; if you only ever contact members of your network when you need something, you're not going to be at the top of their Christmas card list. Relationships should be reciprocal.

Choose your network with care. You become like the people you spend time with (that's why mums say to their kids 'I don't want you hanging around with that lot'), so be selective about who you give your time to, both inside and outside of work. Don't be afraid to ditch the people who constantly whine and are negative; life is too short to drag yourself down. Your close network should comprise people who bring out the best in you, add value to your own thinking and support you. Successful people surround themselves with other successful people, and they're not afraid to learn from them. Make sure you have a 'platinum network' in place: that small group of close contacts whose support you can draw on. And work hard to expand your wider network and connections. It's all about people in the end.

Think win–win

This is really an extension of the 'be a people person' theme, but I think it merits a section of its own. Successful people understand that their success doesn't have to come at the expense of others. Yes, we've all witnessed people who have clambered over and trodden on people on their way to the top, but in my experience it's not a strategy for long-term success. And remember that you're likely to meet those same people on your way down! People who are successful tend to be generous in their approach, and realise that there's plenty of cake for all of us – enough success to go around. In practical terms, this means looking out for other people's interests as well as your own, whether that's in your workplace or your personal life. It means having an approach based on cooperation and collaboration, not competition; it means giving as well as taking. It's about asking, 'What is the best all-round outcome for everyone concerned?' This is the attitude that will win you respect, friends and influence, not enemies and people with grudges against you.

The best mindset is one in which you compete with yourself, not other people. Endlessly comparing yourself with other people is a negative exercise; there will always be people who are more attractive, more popular, richer and, yes, more successful than you. We're all different, we all face different circumstances, and we all have different ideas of what constitutes success, so comparing ourselves with others whose paradigms and goals might be completely different is a waste of time. The only comparison that is really worthwhile is comparing where you are with where you want to be.

Be an action person

Successful people just get on and do things. However positive your attitudes are, nothing's going to happen for you if you don't take action! Action is what will make the difference between getting to where you want to be, and still being where you are five years from now, wondering 'what if'. We've looked already at some of things that hold people back from taking action. The next chapter sets out a whole range of actions and activities that (if you actually do them) will help to contribute to your success.

Chapter 18

The Right Actions

Whether you're looking for a new job, trying to position yourself for promotion, or planning to set up your own business, nothing's going to happen unless you make it happen. Sounds obvious, but you'd be surprised how many people just sit back and wait to get lucky, or for an opportunity to come along. Well, the bad news is, it's unlikely to. But the good news is that there's a huge amount you can do to improve your chances of landing that job, making your business a success or getting that promotion. This chapter sets out the key actions that will help you get closer to your goal, more quickly.

Get organised

Regardless of whether you're looking for a new job, starting a new job and seeking to make a good impact, or planning your own business, your first step should be to get yourself organised. I've said before that you need to approach a job search as a job in itself, and of course the same applies to a business start-up. You've got a lot of work to do, so you need to make sure that you are making the best use of your time. That means two things: you need to focus on the activities that are going to bring you results, and you need to avoid spending time on distractions or unproductive activities. Not exactly rocket science, but something that lots of people fail to grasp or don't take seriously enough. You need to have a focused plan, and you need to make yourself accountable for delivering on that plan.

Before you start putting your action plan together (see below), it's well worth spending some time and effort clearing the ground to give you the space (both physical and mental) to work on your plan. There are three key elements to this:
1 declutter;
2 put a good system in place;
3 learn to manage your time and energy.

Declutter

Whether it's in the office or at home (or probably both), most of us just have too much stuff. And the effect of clutter is entirely negative: it's stressful, it makes us look disorganised (actually, it means that we *are* disorganised), it makes us inefficient and it wastes our time. Clutter is distracting, it saps our energy and affects our concentration. How many times have you spent ages looking for that report/letter/invoice because your desk or cupboards are overflowing with junk you don't need and papers you'll never refer to again? I've heard it estimated that around 80 per cent of the paperwork we file away is never looked at again. Teach yourself to be ruthless: only keep something if you *know* you're going to need it, or if you think you might need it again and you've got the only copy of the document. Otherwise, bin it.

Don't allow yourself to buy in to the old myth that some people work best when their desks are untidy. Nonsense. And think of how you look when your boss comes in to ask you for a copy of that report and then has to wait around while you try to dig it out from underneath the pile of papers on your desk. Or when you waste the first five minutes of a meeting with a prospective client trying to find the paperwork you're looking for on your desk or in your briefcase. Not impressive!

Give yourself a head-start on your career development project, whatever it is, by clearing up before you start. That might mean a couple of hours spent tidying up your office, or a whole weekend clearing your flat and setting up your home office. But do it: it will help you to feel in control, give your motivation a real boost, and clear the decks for you to concentrate on the important stuff. As well as ditching the clutter, tackle those little niggly things that really annoy you: that could be anything from a dripping tap to your tax return. I'm not suggesting that you use all of this as displacement activity to stop you from focusing on, and cracking on with, your career project. What I am saying is that the more distractions and inefficiencies you can eliminate, the faster you'll make progress towards your career objectives, and the more optimistic you'll feel about achieving them.

Put a good system in place

Once you've got rid of all the stuff you don't need, you need an efficient system for dealing with your day-to-day work, as well as your job-search or business development project. It doesn't matter whether your system is paper-based or computerised, as long as it works. One of the best approaches I've come across is set out in David Allen's book *Getting Things Done* (check out the bibliography for more details). His key recommendation is that you have one place (an A4 ring-binder, a file on your computer, or your PDA if you're a real techie) where you keep a note of everything on which you have to take action, whether that's practical things you need to do around the house, work projects you're involved with, or anything else. He suggests that you do a brain-dump of everything that you need to do. (Note: this is a pretty big exercise. It'll probably take you a whole weekend but, trust me, it's worth it). This list then forms the basis for your future action planning. For each item on the list you need to decide what the next steps are and when you need to do them.

The thinking behind this approach is that, if you've written down everything you need to do, you free your mind up to concentrate on whatever task you have in hand, because you're not constantly worrying about all the other things that you mustn't forget to do! It's a simple system, but it works. Of course, you need to make sure that you update your list on a regular basis (perhaps a daily update and then a weekly review), but in my experience the benefits of this approach far outweigh the initial and ongoing effort it takes. You'll feel much more in control, you'll be in a better position to make good decisions about what your priorities are, and you'll be more likely to deal with tasks before they reach crisis point. If you keep your action list with you, you can make much more productive use of those bits of imposed 'downtime' that we all have in a day; you can make phone calls on the train, for example, or catch up on your reading while you're waiting for a meeting to start. Which leads neatly on to the next point...

Learn to manage your time and energy

None of us would have time to read all the books that have been written about time management! Some of the best ones are listed in the bibliography but, in the interests of speed and efficiency, here are some key points on managing your time.

- **It's about managing yourself**. Although we normally talk about time management, the secret to managing our time is really about managing ourselves and our energy. We all have the same amount of time at our disposal, but successful people are better at managing themselves to manage their time. That means being focused, self-disciplined and good at prioritising and planning. It also means recognising the ways in which you work best and arranging your work accordingly. Are you a morning or an evening person, for example? Do you work best in short bursts, or do you prefer to crack on with a task for a couple of hours and then take a longer break? Be aware of your physical, mental and emotional energy levels and patterns, and use those to inform the way in which you plan your working day or week.
- **Prioritise**. The key element of effective time management is knowing what your priorities are. If you don't know that, then you have very little chance of using your time well. If you're self-employed, choosing your priorities is completely down to you, so it's vital to be clear what they are. Know what you absolutely have to achieve today/this week/this month. If you're employed, the most important thing is to be clear what your boss's priorities are. There's no point in spending time on what you think is important if your manager takes a different view. Talk to them regularly. And don't let them get away with saying that everything is a priority! By definition, you can only have one priority at a time. Ask which of the tasks on your list they want you to finish first. And which second, and so on. Of course, there will be plenty of occasions when you're juggling more than one project at a time, but always make sure that you are clear about what is most important and what the deadlines are. Bear in mind that your boss is likely to keep loading you up with stuff until you say 'I can't take any more'. It's your responsibility to let them know when you're at capacity. It's then their responsibility to decide which of the tasks they've given you is the priority.

- **Plan**. Once you know what your priorities and objectives are, you need to put in place a plan to achieve them. To do this, you need to know two things: the deadline for completion of the task, and what the task actually involves. Break the task or project down into its smallest constituent parts. In other words, ask yourself what is the first specific action you need to take. That might be a phone call, or some internet research, or arranging a meeting. Then ask what the next action you need to take is, and so on. Work back from your deadline, allocating sensible amounts of time for each of the steps you have identified (and don't forget to build in some contingency time). And there you have your project plan. Planning isn't rocket science; it's just about being logical, so don't shy away from it. Putting together your plan is the first thing you should do every time you are given (or take on) a new task. (Actually, it's the second thing: the first thing is to determine its level of priority!) Not only does this approach give you a clear path of action, but it's easier to get started if you've broken the task down into a series of small steps, instead of viewing it as one big project.
- **Make sure you spend time on your priorities**. There's no point in putting together a great project plan if you keep allowing yourself to be distracted by trivia. A good way of bringing home to yourself just how easy it is to fritter time away is to carry out a 'time audit'. For one week, keep a diary of exactly how you spend your time, both inside and outside of work. At the end of the week, sit down and compare how you actually spent your time with what you had identified as your professional and personal priorities. I'll bet the results are a bit scary. So, how do you keep yourself on track? Firstly, learn to say 'no' – nicely. If someone asks you to do something, or for help with something, that's not your priority, explain that you're not able to do it. Try to offer them an alternative: perhaps you can do it in a couple of days' time, or maybe you can spend 20 minutes with them to help them get started. (It helps, by the way, if you have your tasks and commitments set out in your diary, so that you can show them you don't have time.) It's much better to be honest than to agree to take on the task and end up working ridiculous hours to complete it, not doing a good job on it, or not delivering on it at all. If it's your boss who's asked you, make them decide on the order of priority. Of course, it's not only other people who divert us from our priorities: most of us are pretty good at doing that for ourselves! Email is one of the biggest time-stealers. Who can resist the temptation of checking what's just popped into the inbox when we hear that little 'ping'? Simple answer: turn the sound off. Discipline yourself to check email only two or three times a day: first thing in the morning, lunchtime and just before you go home. It's not easy, but it makes a big difference to your output. Similarly, don't waste your time on needlessly long telephone conversations, meetings or other distractions. Be clear what you need to get out of the conversation and be focused. Of course you don't want to be brusque or unsociable, but try to get the balance right. Finally, get better at handling paperwork. Most of us handle the same piece of paper up to five times before we

actually deal with it! Use the 3D rule: dump it, delegate it or deal with it. If you can deal with it in two minutes or less, do it now. If not, plan when you are going to deal with it, and put it away until then.

- **Plan your personal time**. This is just as important as planning your work time. Your work is not your life, but it's easy for it to take over. Make a deliberate effort to put things in your diary – a visit to the theatre, a drink with friends – which mean you have to leave the office on time. This will help you to be more efficient in the workplace. If you've got an appointment in your diary, then you have to leave the office at a certain time, so you've simply got to get what you need to do done by a specific deadline. That's why people who have to leave the office at a particular time – to pick their kids up from school, for example – are often some of the most organised and efficient people in a workplace. At this point, if you're a lawyer/banker/management consultant, you'll be saying 'It's all very well for you to tell me to leave the office on time, but I just can't. My workload's far too heavy, and anyway my colleagues/boss would raise their eyebrows.' To which my answer is: is it *really* all about your workload, or about how you manage it? And so what if your colleagues (or boss) disapprove, so long as you are delivering what you need to deliver? Try it: plan to leave the office on time just once in the next two weeks. I promise the world will not fall apart. And try looking at things from a different perspective: people who routinely work excessively long hours are either not up to the job, not organised enough or not sufficiently clear about what their priorities are.
- **Build in thinking time**. Whether it's at the beginning of your working day, at the end, or during, try to include some empty time just for thinking. Many people find meditation helpful, but if that's not your thing, at least make sure you have some quiet time and space for yourself. That might mean going for a walk, or to the gym, or simply getting up half an hour early for a quiet cup of coffee before you start work. This is the time when you're most likely to come up with new ideas, or the answer to the problem that's been nagging you. I've had some of my best ideas in the bath with a glass of wine! Building some space into your day will also help you to keep things in perspective and manage your stress levels better.

Get support

If you've read the chapter on job-search strategies, or the chapter on making an impact, you'll know already that I believe that networking should be a key element of your career strategy. Other people are great short-cuts to the information you need, or the answers to problems that you can't solve yourself. Surrounding yourself with positive, interesting people from a range of walks of life will do more for your knowledge, problem-solving skills and confidence than anything else you spend your time on. As well as the networking tactics we discussed in Chapter 11, here are some more ways to involve other people in helping to move your career forward.

- **Get a mentor**. Who do you know that you view as a real success and respect enormously? Ask them if they'd be prepared to spend a bit of time with you on a regular basis. It doesn't have to be too frequent: maybe once every six weeks, or quarterly. Don't be afraid to ask: most people will be flattered. In any case, successful people will understand the importance of getting support, and will probably themselves have benefited from a mentor in the past. Your mentor doesn't have to be in the same business as you; in fact, often it's better if they work in a completely different industry, as they will bring a fresh perspective. Use your meetings with them to brainstorm ideas, to ask for advice on problems you're facing, and to get some honest feedback on how you're approaching things. Invaluable advice, which will cost you no more than the price of a (nice) lunch.

- **Ask for advice**. Whatever situation you are in or whatever your objectives are, someone, somewhere will have been there before you. Seek them out. You don't have to reinvent the wheel. Most people are happy to talk about themselves and how they succeeded, so draw on the information they have. Don't worry that people will regard you as a threat: they're at a different stage of their career, so that's unlikely. I often get enquiries from people who are hoping to set up their own coaching business, and looking for a little guidance. I'm always happy to give it: I remember all too well what it felt like when I was starting out in business, and I was always profoundly grateful to the people who took the time to give me the benefit of their knowledge and experience. Remember to follow up with people: if they've given you advice, pointers or contacts, get in touch to let them know what happened. Involve them in your development and your success.

- **Cultivate quirky relationships**. The management guru Tom Peters refers to this as putting together a 'freak collection'! A slightly dramatic way of expressing it, perhaps, but the point is a good one. Make sure that your network doesn't consist entirely of people who are just like you. You'll learn much more from people whose perspectives and experience differ from your own. Spending time with different kinds of people will broaden your outlook, give you new ideas and keep your thinking fresh.

- **Recognise the importance of your boss**. If you're employed, your immediate boss is the person with the most influence over your career. They're likely to be the key to your success. This has a couple of implications. Firstly, you need to choose your boss with care! This is more easily said than done, of course, especially if you are moving into a new company or industry, but your research can help here. And don't be afraid of your intuition: if you meet your potential boss at interview, and it doesn't feel right, you may be well advised to listen to those alarm bells. A poor relationship with your boss, and/or a boss who is going nowhere fast in their own career, will do more to stall your career progress than almost anything else. Once you're in your job, make sure that you are delivering what your boss wants, meeting his or her expectations and supporting them in showing themselves in a good light. They're not going to show any loyalty to you if you don't give it to them in the first place.

Keep learning

In the last chapter, we saw how successful people usually have a highly-developed sense of curiosity. Continuing to learn and develop yourself throughout your career is one of the most important ongoing actions you can take. Your attitude to learning helps to determine your future employability. Cultivate lifelong learning; your education doesn't end when you finish university, qualify as a solicitor or get your Masters degree. In fact, a slightly cynical person might say that's when it starts – when you enter the 'real world'!

- **Read widely**. Try to spend half an hour a day reading either inside or outside your subject area. Don't get bogged down by feeling that you have to plough the whole way through a book or article: skim-read, or dip in and out of a book. Often by reading the first and last paragraphs of a chapter you can get the gist of the argument. One thing that's well worth doing is learning how to speed-read; enrol on a course, or read *The Speed Reading Book* by Tony Buzan. Make notes of ideas/issues that interest you, and review your notes every couple of weeks or so. This is a great way of making mental connections you hadn't thought of before and coming up with new ideas and approaches.

- **Work to improve the quality of your thinking**. We all have different thinking styles. Some people are logical thinkers, others are better at blue-skies thinking or brainstorming. Think about the way you think! Focus on making your thinking more inquisitive (keep asking questions), more critical (look for evidence versus assumptions), more strategic (look for the bigger picture), more imaginative (look past the obvious solution) and broader (look for more than one perspective). The good news is that your ability to think is not related to your level of intelligence: anyone can learn to think more effectively. This in turn will help you to deal better with business planning, problem-solving and situations that involve risk or uncertainty.

- **Invest in your development**. You spend money on your clothes, your hair and your appearance generally, so why not spend it on your internal development? Explore what your workplace offers in terms of internal and external training. If the answer is 'not much', sign up for some courses at your own expense and in your own time; you'll take them more seriously if you've had to make that kind of investment. In any case, you don't have to spend a fortune. Lots of organisations offer free or subsidised workshops, or you could check out your local community college, which will have a wide range of courses at very reasonable prices. Don't assume that you should undertake a formal programme like an MBA; instead, think about your skills gaps and the knowledge that will be most useful to you, and plan your ongoing education accordingly.

Keep your eye on the bigger picture

So, you've got yourself organised, you're clear about your priorities and you have a good system for managing your workload. Great: that means that you are giving yourself the best chance of getting things done. Don't, however, allow yourself to make the mistake of losing sight of the bigger picture. It's all too easy to get so tied up with what we're doing on a day-to-day basis that we forget what we're actually doing it *for*. As well as keeping yourself on track on a daily, weekly and monthly basis, it's important to step back every now and then and take a more strategic, long-term view of where you're going. Go back to your big goals and review them regularly. My friends Brett and Debbie Davidson (you can read their case studies at the end of the book) do just this. They lead a busy life: Brett runs his own very successful financial business, helped by Debbie, who is also a professional actress. Twice a year, they take themselves away to a lovely hotel for the weekend, and spend time reviewing their long- and short-term goals. They discuss their plans for the business, set fresh objectives and put holiday breaks in their diary. The result is that they go home re-focused and re-energised, knowing that they have a good professional and personal plan for the next six months. Take a leaf out of Brett and Debbie's book by building regular time into your diary to review your goals and your progress. It's a good idea to get out of your normal surroundings to do this. Take yourself away for a day, or book an afternoon off work and go to your favourite cafe. Here are some suggestions for the kinds of questions to ask yourself.

- What have I achieved in the last six months?
- What have I not achieved that was on my list of goals/priorities? Why?
- What are my three main priorities for the next six months, both professional and personal?
- What commitments do I have to fulfil in the next six months, and when/by when am I going to carry them out?
- What six new activities/approaches am I going to try in the next six months to help my career/business development?
- What am I going to do in the next six months to have fun? When exactly am I going to do these things?

Get on with it!

However much planning and prioritising you do, nothing's going to happen if you don't get out there and make it happen. There comes a point when you just have to take action. I know how big a problem procrastination is for lots of people (myself included), which is why the next chapter focuses entirely on the problem of putting things off, and what to do about it.

Chapter 19

Tackling Procrastination

I've been putting off writing this chapter for ages (only joking!). I decided to devote a whole chapter to the topic of procrastination because experience – my own and my clients' – has shown me that it's the single biggest factor that stops us getting to where we want to be. We simply put off taking the action we need to. There are all sorts of theories about why we procrastinate, but I reckon that ultimately they boil down to one of three key reasons: we don't really want the outcome enough, we don't know how to go about achieving it, or we're scared that we might try but fail. This chapter will help you to deal with whichever of those situations you're finding yourself in.

'I'm just not motivated'

If you just can't seem to be able to get started on that job search, business plan or whatever it is you know you ought to be doing, the first thing to do is to ask yourself why. Your lack of motivation might simply be a sign that you don't really want it that much after all. Maybe you're being pressured by other people to change jobs or set up that business. Get honest with yourself: is it something that you *really* want? How much do you want it? If your heart isn't in it, you're never going to be able to motivate yourself to do anything concrete about it. Worse, you'll end up feeling bad/guilty/demoralised because you haven't achieved anything.

If you're struggling to get going with taking action, sit down and answer these questions honestly.

- How much do I really want this?
- Am I doing it for me, or to live up to someone else's expectations?
- What will be the benefit to me if I achieve this?
- What will be the cost to me of achieving it?
- Do I feel excitement or dread when I think about the change I'm contemplating?
- Am I doing this because I want to do it, or because I feel I should do it?

If you can put your hand on your heart and say that you really do want to make the change, then read on to find out how to tackle your procrastination. But if deep down you know that you're really not that hungry for it after all, then it's back to the drawing board. There's no point at all in making the effort to change your career or your circumstances if your heart isn't in it. Go back to your values and goals exercises. Think again about what you really, really want. Without a sense of excitement, you'll never motivate yourself, and you'll end up in a downward spiral of negativity, feeling guilty about not taking action. The spark has to be there in the first place.

'I don't know how'

I often work with clients who know what they want to do, but can't seem to work out a plan to get there. In my experience, their problem often stems from the fact that they haven't broken their plan down into steps that are small and simple enough. Thinking 'I'm going to set up my own business' is daunting. It's a huge leap. But if you take it a small step at a time, it suddenly seems a lot more manageable. So your very first step might be to get together with friends to brainstorm some business ideas. Or, if you know what you want to do, your first step might be spending a couple of hours on the internet researching the competition. A really good question to ask yourself is: 'What is the first single action I need to take?' It could be something as simple as buying a notebook to write your business plan in. Work out the very first thing you need to do. Then just do it. Then work out the very next thing you need to do. And just do it. Commit yourself to doing just one thing each day – your 'single daily action' – to take you closer to your goal, and chances are you'll find that your momentum and motivation start to take off and take over. Don't terrify yourself into inaction by looking at the enormity of your task: take it one step at a time. Take this book, for example: the prospect of writing 75,000 words is scary. How can someone ever get that done? But by tackling it a chapter at a time, gradually the words mount up. It's the same for any project: broken down into its constituent parts, it's a lot more manageable.

'What if I fail?'

This one again! Fear of failure is one of the biggest causes of procrastination. It's easier to live the fantasy than to take action and risk things not working out as we'd hoped. If we never start something, then by definition we can't fail. Equally, if we don't put in enough (or any) effort, then we've given ourselves the perfect excuse if we do fail ('I wasn't really trying'). Remember, failure is a given. It happens to everyone. And it's the best learning technique there is. Go back and read Chapters 9 and 17 again. And then get over it and get on with it.

What if you still can't get going?

What do you do if you know that you want to make the change, you know how to go about it, and the prospect of failing doesn't terrify you, but you still can't seem to get going? I'm afraid the brutal answer here is: just get on with it! Every change we want to make will involve uncomfortable elements. We want our business to be more successful, for example, but we dread the thought of making those sales calls. The only thing that will bring results is action, so here are the best ways to cajole yourself into taking those first steps.

- **Keep your goal and outcome in sight**. Keep the picture of where you want to end up clearly in your head to boost your motivation. Imagine how good it will feel when you're hosting the party for your book launch (yes, I've been using that trick), or when you've got that promotion. See yourself where you want to be.
- **Be clear about your priorities on a daily basis**. You can't do everything at once, so don't write yourself a two-page to-do list: know which three key actions you need to take today and focus on achieving those. Break tasks down into their smallest possible components. Plan exactly what you're going to do and when; write it in your diary, however small a task it is. Then you know what time you're going to do it and you can tick it off the list when it's done.
- **Do the worst thing first**. This technique works well whether you're trying to have a productive day in the office, or you're focusing on your job search or developing your business. Getting that task you're dreading out of the way first thing will make everything you do that day seem much easier, and you won't have the dread of it hanging over you all day. You'll zoom through everything else.
- **Just do five minutes**. Tell yourself you'll just work on the task for five minutes. Then work on the task for five minutes. Chances are, you'll find you've got yourself on a bit of a roll and you'll keep going. If not, hey, at least you've done five minutes' worth.
- **Bribe yourself!** Tell yourself that if you make five phone calls, you can spend half an hour surfing the internet for fun, or if you finish that report you'll knock off early and go for a drink. Acknowledge the progress you're making: don't just keep looking ahead at everything you still have to do. My technique for writing this book has been to say, 'I'll write 2,000 words a day'. If I get them done by lunchtime, I stop. If it takes me till 7pm, then so be it. The motivation for me is to get the 2,000 words written so that I can do other things.
- **Get other people involved**. Agree a task and its deadline with your partner or a friend. Finish your business plan by the end of the week and they'll buy you dinner. Fail to finish it, and dinner's on you!

Remember: it's you who has to take action. It's no one else's responsibility.

Part 4
Doing Your Own Thing

Chapter 20

Is Entrepreneurialism for Me?

Many of the clients who come to me for career coaching are attracted to the idea of setting up their own business. It's not surprising: if you're feeling fed up and disillusioned with the corporate world, it's a natural progression to think about doing your own thing. But that's about as far as most people get. Sometimes people have had a business idea but never seem to get round to doing anything about it. Other people think that they would love to set up their own business, but aren't sure what to do.

I am a firm believer that everyone should, at some point in their lives, think about setting up their own business. It's fun and exciting, it's a completely different experience from the corporate world, and it's a terrific learning opportunity. There is a whole range of business models that you can adopt, from making a bit of extra money in addition to your main job, through to setting up a scaleable business that will earn you a really good living in its own right. This section of the book is aimed at the budding entrepreneur and covers the key things you need to consider if you're thinking about going it alone: coming up with your business idea, writing your business plan and marketing your business. It doesn't claim to be a comprehensive guide to every single detail that you will need to deal with, but the bibliography contains further resources to help you.

First of all, though, let's take a look at the benefits of an entrepreneurial lifestyle, and the qualities you'll need to succeed at building your own business.

The benefits

First and foremost, it's about lifestyle. Running your own business gives you the opportunity to spend your time doing something that you are passionate about. It also gives you an enormous amount of control over what you do, how you do it, and how long you spend doing it. And it gives you the opportunity to earn money for yourself, not for someone else!

Lots of people who fancy the idea of setting up their own business are put off by the perception that they're going to end up working 24 hours a day, seven days a week. And there's no point in denying that it's hard work. But the bottom line is that it's for you to decide what you want to put into – and get out of – your business. When we think of an entrepreneur, we usually have an image of Richard

Branson, Alan Sugar, Anita Roddick: people who have made millions doing their own thing. But there are also thousands of people in the UK who make extremely good livings through their own businesses without ever hitting the dizzy heights of millionaire status. Not every business-owner wants to scale their business up to become a household name or a multinational brand. Some people choose to set up on their own because it gives them benefits other than, or as well as, money: flexibility, freedom or control, for example. It's about lifestyle choice.

The first thing you should do if you are contemplating your own business is to ask yourself, 'Why do I want this?' Look back at your values exercise. How well does the lifestyle of an entrepreneur fit with what's really important to you? There are no right or wrong answers to why you might want to go it alone, but I would say that if money is your main motivation, you might want to have a bit of a rethink. Yes, you might well be very successful, but it's likely to take time, energy and risk, so it's not the easiest way to make a living. If, on the other hand, you are attracted by the autonomy and excited about the very direct link between your effort and the rewards you could reap, then it could well be the right path for you.

Qualities of an entrepreneur

In Chapter 7, we looked briefly at some of the questions you need to ask yourself if you're thinking about setting up in business. To recap, in my own and my clients' experience, the key attributes that you need if you're going to make a go of it include the following.

- **Common sense**. In spades. You need to be able to look objectively at your business idea and see if it's really a 'go-er', and be honest with yourself about the prospects of turning your fantasy into reality. (You'll need to do lots of research, too, as we discuss later, but a common-sense approach should be your starting point.)
- **Self-discipline**. The only person who can make your business a success is you, so you're going to have to do most, if not all, of the work. You'll have to have the discipline to get started and to keep going, even if things don't seem to be going too well or are taking longer than you anticipated.
- **Resilience**. Similarly, you're going to need the strength of character to deal with setbacks and disappointments, which will definitely happen. You'll need to be good at finding your way around obstacles, changing tack if something doesn't quite work out as planned, and dealing with rejection.
- **Creativity**. This isn't just about coming up with your business idea in the first place; it's also about how you market and sell it, how you differentiate yourself from your competitors, and how you deal with those obstacles that will arise. The best business people are those who can continually spot new opportunities or ways of refining their product or service, so that they stay one step ahead of the competition.
- **Selling skills**. It goes without saying that you need to be able, and prepared, to

sell. Whether you're offering a product or a service, you'll have to persuade your potential customers that they really want what you have to offer. More about this later, but at this stage you need to get comfortable with the idea that you will have to promote yourself, and not everyone will want to buy.

If you're still reading, I'm assuming that you reckon you've got, or can further develop, these skills. Your first real challenge, then, is coming up with your business idea. That's the subject of the next chapter.

Chapter 21

Your Business Idea

As I've already said, I've come across plenty of clients who say that they are keen to set up their own businesses. Their sticking point is that they don't know what their business could be! Here are a couple of key points to remember at the outset.

- **Very few business ideas are completely new**. Chances are there is someone out there doing something similar to what you might be contemplating. That's fine; competition is a good thing, because it shows that a market exists for the product or service. What you need to come up with is a way of differentiating your product. Why will people buy from you and not from someone else? The two ways of differentiating are on the grounds of price and quality. Generally speaking, it's better to focus on the quality side of things. Ask yourself, 'How can I do this better?' If your only differentiator is price, you're going to have to undercut the competition, which has an obvious knock-on effect on your bottom line. And it's often difficult, if not impossible, for the small guy to undercut the bigger player, because they can operate economies of scale that you won't have.

- **It's best to stick with something you know**. Trying to enter an industry sector about which you know nothing is setting yourself a big challenge, especially if you're looking for investment: potential investors will be keen to see evidence that you know your market. Research can help to an extent, but nothing beats hands-on experience. That's why many entrepreneurs set up their own consultancy company, based on the skills and experience that they have gained during their corporate life. Of course, if you've come up with a truly groundbreaking idea (but see above!), then this route won't be open to you. You'll have to compensate for this with the quality of your market research.

So how do you go about finding your business idea? Here are some effective techniques.

- **Start with your interests**. Revisit your interests exercise and look at your interests from a potential business perspective. Do you have hobbies that might translate into business opportunities? What subjects and issues really interest you, and is there a way you could make money from them by sharing your knowledge? What problems have you had sourcing materials, advice or opportunities to do the things you like to do in your spare time? Is there a business possibility here? Check out online forums and chat sites relevant to your hobbies or other issues that interest you. What points get raised again and again? What does that tell you about possible business opportunities? (Do bear in mind, though, that many of your hobbies will be things that you only want to do in your spare time, and making a business out of them could take away most of the pleasure you get out of them, so think carefully about this option.)

- **Remember why people buy**. Customers buy products or services for one of two reasons: either they solve a problem, or they increase pleasure. So think about problems that you or your peer group have encountered, and what the solutions to them might be. That's how I came up with my idea for a career coaching business. I had left the world of politics and didn't know what to do next. Although I'd read careers books, I still felt really unclear about my future direction. And then I thought, 'I can't be the only person who is facing this problem; lots of people don't like their jobs or don't know what to do with their lives.' And so the idea for City Life Coaching was born. I would work with young professionals who wanted to change career, improve their prospects or get a better work–life balance. My business idea came directly from my own problem.

- **Stay curious**. Observe the world around you, read avidly and look for new connections (both people and ideas). Keep your eye out for new industry trends or patterns of consumer behaviour. What's happening in the world of business, politics and society generally that could give you an opening? For example, one of the Government's biggest priorities is tackling obesity. And when central Government has a priority, it makes money available. For someone passionate about health and wellbeing, that could open up all sorts of new opportunities for advising on nutrition and lifestyle, or feeding families healthily on a budget.

- **Brainstorm**. Sit down with friends and just throw some ideas around. Other people's ideas will prompt more of your own. Write everything down to analyse later; all sorts of new suggestions could leap out at you.

If you are still struggling to come up with an idea of your own, there are other routes into self-employment that might be worth considering. These include franchising, or buying into an existing business. The benefits are obvious: the business and its brand are already established, and you'll have support and advice to draw on. But there are downsides, too: if your reason for going into business on your own is because you want lots of autonomy, you might find the bureaucracy and standardisation that a franchise entails stifling. Similarly, if you go into business with someone else, either by buying a stake in an existing company or setting up in partnership with someone who has had a good idea, you're not going to have the degree of freedom that you would if you were the sole proprietor. Again, it helps if you are very clear about what you hope to achieve from the business.

Some final questions

Even once you've come up with your business idea, there are a few more questions you need to ask yourself before you get into the detailed planning stage. Basically, you need to be as sure as you can not only that the idea is a good one, but that it is a good one for you. Ask yourself the following questions.

- **Is this something that I am best placed to do?** Do I have the right skills and experience? If not, how long is it going to take me to acquire them?
- **How interested am I in this, really?** There's no written rule that says you have to be totally passionate about what your business does, but you do need to be passionate about making it work, and that's easier if you have a real interest in the product or service. In any case, it's more likely that you'll have come up with your idea as a result of thinking about something that you know about or are interested in.
- **Is the timing right?** As we know, there's seldom a perfect time for anything, but there's no point in stacking the odds against yourself. So think about your personal and financial circumstances, as well as the shape of the market. Is the time right, not just for the product or service, but for you personally? This isn't intended to give you an excuse to procrastinate! But it is important to take a realistic view of your current situation.

If you've got this far through the process and you're still excited, then it's time to do some more detailed planning.

Chapter 22

Your Business Plan

The words 'business plan' seem to strike terror into the heart of many an aspiring entrepreneur. I guess it's the numbers thing! And, if you've ever watched the television series 'Dragons' Den', where entrepreneurs pitch their business idea to a panel of experts, you'll know that most people fall apart, often excruciatingly, when it comes to detailed scrutiny of their financial forecasts. But the good news is that business planning doesn't have to be a terrifying process. It's really about two things: research and reality. Research, because you need to know your potential market and exactly why customers will buy your product and service as opposed to someone else's (or none at all); reality, because most people massively over-estimate how much money they're going to bring in, and how quickly.

What's a business plan actually *for*? Obviously, if you're seeking outside investment for your business you need to be able to explain to the potential investor what you're planning to do and, just as importantly, how you're going to make money from it, and what the investor's return is going to be (there's more about this in Chapter 24). But, first and foremost, your business plan is for you. It's your tool for making sure that you've taken account of everything you need to in planning your start-up. Most importantly of all, remember that a business plan isn't a static document: it's a work-in-progress, which you will need to refine and revise as your thinking (and your business) develops.

So let's demystify the business-planning process. (There are lots of free resources available that can help you. Most high-street banks, for example, offer a free business-planning guide, or even software that provides a template for you to fill in. And free advice is available from a range of Government and other agencies, including BusinessLink and the National Federation of Enterprise Agencies. Bear in mind, however, that at the end of the day the person who knows most about your business plan is you, so the onus is on you to make sure that it's comprehensive but accessible.)

Basically, there are five key questions that you need to be able to answer in putting your plan together.

- **What am I selling?** (Your product.)
- **To whom am I selling it?** (Your customers.)
- **Why will they buy from me and not from someone else (or not at all)?** (Your differentiator.)
- **How am I going to reach them?** (Your marketing strategy.)
- **What will they be prepared to pay?** (Your pricing strategy.)

What am I selling, and to whom?

You need to answer these two questions together. Without a product or service, you obviously won't have customers; but, equally, without customers, there's no point in having a product or service! So as soon as you've come up with your business idea, you need to know to whom you're selling. It's really important to be clear about your market segment, or niche: to whom *exactly* are you selling? You might define that on the basis of a geographical area, or on the basis of the customer demographic: young professionals, or people considering a gap year, for example. In my experience, the better defined your potential customer base is, the easier you will find it to market to them (see the marketing section below). It's much harder to try to market to 'the general public'. So think about who is most likely to find your idea useful, and what their needs are. In my own business, I focus on providing career coaching to young professionals. I've found it much easier to market that service than a wider service offering life coaching to anyone who needs it, because it's easier not only to identify my potential customers, but to target my marketing to reach them.

Don't think only in terms of the product or service you are offering; you need to think about what the *benefits* of it are to the customer. What problem are you solving for them, or what additional experience are you offering them? Again, to use my own business as an example, the benefit that I offer is that I help people to decide what career they really want, and to make the change. So my target market is young professionals who are unhappy at work, and there are plenty of them!

Now you need to do some more detailed research. If your friends and family think that your idea is a runner, that's a good start, but it's not enough. You need to have as much evidence as possible that your product or service will actually sell. Start off with some internet research. Is there an existing market (that is, are other people selling something similar)? If not, why not? Is there already something similar in your area? A small town might be able to provide enough business for another restaurant or bistro, for example, but it's less likely to be able to support another secondhand bookshop if the high street already has one. So look for competition that shows the market is healthy, but be wary of competition that is too close at hand. If there's no competition at all, tread carefully: either you've come up with a stunningly original idea (possible, but quite unlikely), or other people have tried the same thing before you and discovered to their cost that there's no market for it (much more likely).

You also need to estimate how big your potential market is. There's no point in delivering a service that only 20 people in the country will want to buy (unless they're paying you thousands of pounds for it, of course!). How many people are likely to be interested in what you have to offer? And will their purchases be one-offs, or is there the potential for repeat business, or follow-up sales of complementary products or services? The starting point is to find out how big the existing market is for your product or similar products, and make as realistic an estimate as you can of the share of that market that you might hope to obtain. This will depend partly on the **structure** of the market: does it consist of a few big players, or lots of small independents? It could be easier to break into the latter, as the big players will always be able to operate economies of scale that you can't. On the other hand, you might be able to differentiate yourself from the big players by offering something better, quicker, or with a higher standard of customer service. It will also depend, of course, on the nature of your product or service: for example, whether it is something very niche (in which case you might aim to become the market leader), or whether it is something that is widely in demand (in which case you might do very well with only a small proportion of the total market share). Either way, you need to have as realistic a projection as possible of the impact you can make.

Once you've gathered as much information as you can from desk research, back it up with some field research. Get out there and ask people what they think. You could talk to existing contacts in the business world, or to people who are doing something similar but are further ahead in their business (yes, they will often be prepared to talk to you). Use online forums or chat rooms to canvass opinion. Use every means you can to get as balanced and rounded a view of your idea as possible.

There are two caveats: firstly, especially if you think your idea is unique, be careful how much detail you give away if you are talking to a stranger. You wouldn't want them to nick your idea and get it to market more quickly! Equally, recognise that all the advice you get is simply other people's perspectives: you are likely to know more about the detail of the business than they are, so don't necessarily be put off by a few negative comments. That said, if the majority of the feedback you get is negative, then the alarm bells should be ringing.

Why will customers buy from me and not from someone else?

Your plan needs to set out clearly how you are going to differentiate yourself from the competition. Will you be cheaper, quicker, more professional, higher quality or more niche? What do your competitors do that you can improve on? What are your competitors not offering that customers would like or benefit from? As I've said already, if your only differentiating factor is that you are cheaper, you might want to think again (unless there is a unique reason for your cheapness; for example, perhaps you can operate without premises, which allows you to undercut the competition). In general, a price war is not a situation you want to be in, as the only thing you can do to keep competing is to keep cutting prices, and thus your profits.

Get as clear as you can about the basis on which your potential customers will make their buying decisions. Customers will always make a trade-off in their mind between the quality of what they are getting and the price they are willing to pay. What does your research indicate about the kinds of features that customers will pay more for? How will they compare you with the competition, and which are the criteria that really matter to them?

Check out the competition thoroughly. Get hold of their marketing material, brochures and company reports if you can. Do an internet search to see what other people – customers, business commentators – are saying about them. Ring them up and pretend to be a potential customer (there's nothing wrong with a little bit of industrial espionage!). How did you rate your customer experience? What would you have done better or differently?

And think widely about who your competition really is. It might not be limited simply to companies who are offering something similar to you, but to those that are offering something that seems quite different, but fulfils the same need. So, for example, if you are planning on setting up an online wine and chocolates gift distribution service, your competitors are not just other wine and chocolate retailers, but anyone who sells items that make great gifts. In fact, in many cases you are competing with anyone who is selling something that people spend their disposable income on; customers only have so much money to spend, so they will make spending decisions based on their personal priorities and preferences. Think about ways in which you can get your product or service to the top of that list.

You also need to be alert to circumstances outside your control that could affect your business's viability. For example, new regulations about the provision of financial services might affect your plans for a financial consultancy business, or consumers' increasing awareness of health and nutrition issues could have an impact on your plans for a fast-food bar. So carry out what's known as a PEST analysis: look at the political, economic, societal and technological landscape, and be alert to new developments that might be relevant to your business plan. You'd be well advised to do this on a regular, ongoing basis, by the way: Government policy, economic conditions and consumer attitudes can all change remarkably quickly. This doesn't have to be as time-consuming as you might think. Signing up to a few publications and websites will do a lot of the work for you (assuming you read them, of course!). I'm a fan of the *Economist*, and in particular its subsidiary publications like *Intelligent Life* and *The World in 2008*. Websites such as www.trendwatching.com are full of useful trend information, as well as fodder for your marketing plans.

How am I going to reach my customers?

There are literally thousands of books about marketing on the market. (Some really good ones are listed in the bibliography). But, in a phrase, the secret to successful marketing is this: know your customer. The clearer you are about your potential customers, and the more you know about their lifestyles and purchasing habits, the easier it will be to market to them. Which publications do they read? Which internet sites do they frequent? Where do they shop? Where do they eat out or spend their leisure time? What level of disposable income are they likely to have and what do they spend it on? All of this information will give you valuable clues about the most effective marketing strategy for your business. Many start-up businesses don't have lots of money available for marketing, and in fact it's all too easy to throw money at a marketing or advertising campaign for little return. So it's a good discipline to think about ways in which you can promote your product at little or no cost. There are plenty of ideas in Chapter 25.

How much are my customers going to pay?

You need to have a reasonable estimate of the size of your target market, and to what proportion of it you are likely to be able to market successfully; but you also need to know what they're prepared to pay. Again, check out the competition. You don't want to price yourself out of the market by charging twice as much as anyone else (unless there are features of your offering that genuinely justify it, of course), but nor do you want to underprice your services. People generally believe that quality has a price-tag attached, and will be wary of pricing that seems too good to be true. And, of course, if it is too good to be true, you're unlikely to make any money!

Once you're really clear about the answers to these five questions, you've got the basis of your business plan: what you're going to sell, to whom and for how much. But, in order to estimate your cashflow and profits, you also need to know what your costs, both start-up and ongoing, are going to be. In the next chapter, we'll look at this, as well as the other practical issues you need to address.

Pulling it all together

Once you've got the answers to the questions above, you need to pull them together into a short, two- or three-sentence summary: your 'elevator pitch'. This should describe, succinctly and accurately, what you do and what is special about it. Take time to craft these sentences carefully; they will be the first thing that potential investors read in your plan, and they will also form the core of your marketing approach. After all, if you can't describe what you offer briefly and compellingly, why should anyone buy from you?

Chapter 23

The Practicalities

This is the boring bit, but don't be tempted to skip it. You need to get the basics right. This chapter flags up the main areas that you need to consider, but I don't claim that it's comprehensive, and it's well worth getting some expert advice on any issues you aren't sure about. (There's a list of relevant resources at the end of the book). The one thing you do not want to do under any circumstances is fall foul of the law; you'll end up tangled in red tape and it could be disastrous for your business.

Name/logo

One of the first things you'll want to think about is a name for your business. This is important because it's obviously a key part of your branding. That said, if you're not careful, you can end up spending hours of your time (and even lots of money) coming up with your business name and logo; time and money that could be spent more effectively elsewhere. Broadly, there are three main approaches you can adopt.

1   Use your own name. This can sound professional and established (depending on your name of course!). Think brands like Marks and Spencer, McDonalds, Woolworths.
2   Use a descriptive name. Think Pizza Express (pizza served quickly), Vision Express (glasses provided quickly) and so on.
3   Use a random name: think Google or Amazon. You can't tell what the business is from its name, but that hasn't stopped these brands from being phenomenally successful; 'google' has even become a verb that means 'to search on the web'.

On balance, I prefer the descriptive approach. It's clear to your customers what you do (or roughly what you do), and your business name is likely to be more memorable. Here are some more tips.

● Don't choose a name that limits you too much in terms of what you offer; you might decide to develop your business in a range of ways over the years, so leave yourself some flexibility.
● Choose a name that is fairly short, or can be easily and logically abbreviated. Your business name should also be your website domain name, and you don't want anything that is going to take ages to type, or is likely to be misspelt.
● Don't choose anything too cheesy or cliched, although if you can come up with a very clever pun, that can be a successful approach.

One of the best ways to come up with a name for your business is to brainstorm ideas with friends. Explain to them what your business will be, pour them a glass of wine, and let the ideas flow!

Once you've come up with a name, you need to check that no one is using it already. This is pretty straightforward. Firstly, check out your chosen name on the Companies House website (www.companieshouse.gov.uk), which lists all the incorporated companies in the UK. It doesn't, however, list businesses that are operating on a sole trader basis (see below), but if you type your chosen name into some of the main search engines, you'll see whether anyone has registered your name as a web address. If they have, choose another name, as you'll need the right domain name for your website. The best domain names are ones ending in '.com', or '.co.uk' if your business will only be targeting the UK market. You can also check out the National Business Register (www.start.biz), which allows you to conduct free searches of business names, companies, trade marks and domain names.

Trading status

You need to decide whether you're going to operate as a sole trader, a partnership or a limited company. There are pros and cons to each of these approaches. For example, the simplest approach is to register yourself as a sole trader; all you need to do is notify HM Revenue and Customs (formerly the Inland Revenue). However, if you intend to do business with other large companies, there's an advantage to setting yourself up as a limited company (incorporating), as it does make you look more professional. HMRC publishes a free guide to starting up in business, and its website contains lots more detailed information on your trading status options (www.hmrc.gov.uk). It's also worth taking the advice of an accountant, as different tax rules apply to each kind of status and, depending on your projected turnover and profit, one form of trading may be more advantageous to you than another.

My broad advice would be, in the first instance, to adopt the trading status that is most straightforward. It's easy to set up as a sole trader, and equally easy to convert into a limited company at a later date if that is more appropriate. In the early days, you want to be spending as much time as possible building your business rather than dealing with regulations and paperwork, so keep it as simple as you can.

Tax

If your business is making money then (sadly, I know) you are going to have to pay tax on your profits. The way in which you pay tax will be determined by your trading status, but the most important thing for you to do (apart from taking some professional advice) is to keep good records from the outset. You need to record every purchase and sale you make. There is a lot of good accounting software on the market to make this easier. Make sure that you keep your records up-to-date, so that you know exactly where you are in terms of profit and cashflow at any point in time.

You can do your own book-keeping, or get someone to help you with it. If you adopt the latter approach, though, don't make the mistake of thinking you can absolve yourself of the responsibility of knowing what financial state your business is in. You need to keep on top of this; it's your money after all! Do get an accountant to help you with your tax return at the end of the year. They will be much more savvy than you about what you can (and can't) legitimately claim as expenses, for example, and their advice is likely to save you more money than their fee will cost you.

VAT

If your projected turnover is more than £64,000 (at the time of writing), then you will need to register for VAT (value-added tax). This is an indirect tax on expenditure, normally charged at 17.5 per cent (some products and services have lower ratings, and a few are exempted altogether). If your turnover is less than this, you can still register voluntarily if you think it is in your interests to do so. For example, if you are manufacturing a product, then if you are VAT registered you will be able to claim back the VAT that you pay on your supplies. But you will also have to charge your customers VAT. If you are providing a service mainly to individual clients who will not be able to claim back the VAT because they are not operating as a business (for example, if you are a personal trainer), then you are effectively adding the best part of 20% to their bill. If, on the other hand, most of your clients are other businesses, they will be VAT registered and will be able to claim back the VAT element of your bill.

Again, there is an argument that being registered for VAT makes you look more credible and professional. However, my advice would be to hang fire on registering for VAT – unless you have to – until your business is up and running properly. It's one more piece of admin that you can probably do without.

Again, for detailed information, visit the HMRC website, speak to your accountant, or book a place on one of the many free courses offered by the Government. These cover a whole range of financial and other business issues for start-ups (find details at www.businessadviceday.gov.uk).

Bank account

Legally, you don't have to have a separate business bank account. That said, many banks include in the small print of their terms and conditions the requirement that you don't use a personal account for business purposes. And in practice it's much easier to keep an eye on your business finances if they are separate from your personal expenditure.

Shop around to find the best business banking deal that you can. Obviously, this will be dictated by your personal requirements and priorities. Criteria to consider when you are choosing your business bank include: the level of charges, whether there is an overdraft facility, how convenient it will be for you to deposit and withdraw funds, and how much business support/advice they offer.

Insurance

Depending on the nature of your business, you might need to consider taking out various kinds of insurance. For example, if you are offering a service based on your advice and expertise, you should consider taking out professional indemnity insurance to protect yourself against possible damages claims from clients. If you are employing staff, you must have employers' liability insurance (in case one of your employees injures themselves as a result of your negligence, for example). If you have premises, you'll need insurance against fire and theft.

This probably all sounds a bit depressing, but it's much better to be safe than sorry. Again, get some legal advice to make sure that you are not spending money on premiums for insurance cover that will be of little value to you.

Premises

Whether you need premises will depend mainly on the kind of business you are setting up. If your business is a consultancy or advice service, for example, which involves you going out to meet clients, you might not need an office at all, as you could work from home and meet clients either at their own premises or on neutral territory, such as an upmarket hotel. Working from home is also ideal if you are planning an online business, although, depending on what you're selling, you might need to rent storage space for stock. There are obvious advantages to working from home: it's cheaper, you don't have a commute, and you can do the laundry in your lunch-break, for example. Of course there are downsides too: you might be short of space, you need to take account of the effect of your business activities on your neighbours, and you'll need a lot of self-discipline to stay away from daytime television. If you do decide that you can work from home, check with your mortgage lender or landlord and your local authority that there are no restrictions on your doing so.

If you decide that you need to lease office premises, shop around. Try to avoid getting tied into a long lease; some office-space providers now offer serviced offices with leases as short as three months. Some local authorities make 'business incubator' space available to start-up businesses, so do check out that option. It might also be possible to sub-let space from another company. And don't forget to use your contacts to get news of any available space by word-of-mouth.

If your business is selling a product that you need or want to showcase physically (not just online), there are still ways in which you can do this cheaply. For example, you might be able to avoid the expense of premises by 'piggy-backing' on someone else, perhaps by persuading local retailers or other businesses to stock your items. Or, if you are selling upmarket items like jewellery or fashion, you could follow the trend that has sprung up recently for 'exclusive' parties, where you invite potential customers to your home for champagne, nibbles and a private shopping experience. Even if you intend to lease premises at some point, tactics like this can be a great way of dipping your toe in the water and testing the market before you commit yourself completely.

Of course, there are some businesses for which premises are a prerequisite: bars and restaurants, for example. If your business is of this sort, location will be a key criterion. Don't rush into a decision; take time to check out what other types of business are in the vicinity and to measure daily footfall – how many people in your target market actually pass by every day.

The bottom line is: don't spend money on infrastructure unless you have to. Be imaginative in thinking about ways in which you can sell your product or service without having to lease space to do so, at least for your first period of trading, while you test the market.

Once you've decided how you're going to deal with these practicalities, you're well on your way. There's probably still one thing holding you back, though: how are you going to fund your business?

Chapter 24

Funding Your Business

How you fund your business depends to a very large extent on what your business is. You need to think about what your start-up and running costs will be, and what your income will be (i.e., how much you will sell). So the first step is to work out those figures. This is the financial section of your business plan, and it's critical.

Projected costs

The easiest place to start is with your costs, because you should be able to estimate these pretty accurately. Basically, you'll have two kinds of costs: direct and indirect. Indirect costs are those costs that relate to the business but are not affected by how much business you do. These include:

- premises;
- equipment;
- insurance;
- stationery;
- marketing budget;
- travel costs; and
- advisors – accountants, lawyers, etc.

We've looked at most of these already (and we'll discuss marketing in the next chapter), but the golden rule is to keep your costs as low as possible without sacrificing quality. It's also an extremely good idea to build a contingency element into your budget, for unexpected costs.

Don't forget to factor in the cost of yourself. How much money do you need to live on every month? Even if you're planning on living off your savings in the first instance, you still need to include your living costs in your calculations so that you can work out how much business you have to do in order to be able to survive.

Also, remember that you will have to pay tax! As a guideline, you'll need to put aside around a third of your profits to cover your tax bill.

If you are providing a service, your indirect costs (or overheads) and your cost of living should be your only expenditure. If you're making and/or selling a product, then you will also have to take account of the 'direct' or purchase cost of the materials or the product. You also need to include the cost of the time it takes to make/package/deliver the product. You might be doing it yourself in the first instance, but if your business is to be sustainable and capable of growth, you have to be able to make a profit from what you're selling after you've paid for the materials and the cost of someone else's labour to produce it for you. A recent example on the television show 'Dragons' Den' illustrates this point. A couple had gone into business making Caribbean ready meals. They had secured contracts with two major supermarkets and the products were flying off the shelves. However, they had outsourced the production of the meals to another manufacturer and, by the time they had paid that supplier's charges, as well as packaging and delivery costs, they weren't actually making any profit at all. They had failed to take proper account of the cost of someone else producing the product for them. What they needed to do was to negotiate a better deal with the supplier, or increase the retail price.

Projected sales

Once you know your costs, you can work out the minimum amount of business you must do to bring in the money to cover them: your break-even point. Of course, you don't just want to break even! The whole idea of business is to make a (preferably nice, healthy) profit. How much do you have to sell to do that?

This is probably the hardest part of your business plan. When you're estimating your costs, you have a lot of hard data to work with: you know – or can find out – what your office rent, stationery bill, IT costs etc are likely to be. It's much harder accurately to estimate how much money you're going to be able to bring in. This is where you need to go back to your marketing plan.

At this stage your sales forecasts can only ever be estimates, but you must base them on as much concrete evidence and information as you can, and you absolutely *must* avoid over-estimating your likely sales. Returning to the 'Dragons' Den' again, the most common mistake that entrepreneurs pitching to the Dragons make is wildly over-estimating the sales they will achieve, and therefore the value of the business. And everyone who does this gets a roasting from the Dragons! So err on the side of conservatism. If you do better than you expect, it will be a nice surprise!

Go back to your market research. What is the size of your target market? What percentage of that market does it seem reasonable for you to be able to capture? What evidence do you have that people will actually buy from you? How long is it likely to take to get each customer, and are you looking at one-off sales or repeat purchases? How long is it likely to take you to build up your customer base? How many customers will you actually be able to serve? (This is especially important if you are planning a service business; you won't be able to spend all your time delivering your service, as you'll have travel time, admin time, selling time and so on, so don't over-estimate how many customers you can cope with.) How much money will you make from each sale, and how much profit after you have subtracted your direct costs? Remember that you also have to cover your indirect costs too, and you can't regard yourself as having made any real (net) profit until you've done that.

It will probably be difficult for you to get hard evidence to back up your assumptions, but you must do the best you can. Particularly if you are seeking outside investment (see below), you will need to be able to demonstrate that there really is a market for your business.

If this all seems like a heck of a lot of work: it is. But you have to be as sure as you can be that you are actually going to be able to make money from your business venture. And, if you're looking for outside investment, you need to be able to convince other people too. We'll look at this next.

Funding your business

As I said above, the amount and nature of funding that you'll need depends on the nature of your business. For example, if you're planning to set up a consultancy service, then you'll need money to cover your indirect costs and your living costs, but that's about it. If, on the other hand, you're planning to open a bar or produce snowboards, you'll need a much higher level of capital investment upfront. That's when you'll most probably have to turn to other people. This section looks at the different ways in which you can fund your business, starting with situations in which your financial requirement is low, and working up to situations where you need substantial investment.

- **Use your savings**. This is the obvious and ideal situation. Clearly, it's only viable if you have a significant level of savings and/or if your start-up and running costs are not too high (as in a service business, for example). But, if you are going to need to borrow money from other lenders or investors, bear in mind that they will want to see a high level of personal and financial commitment from you, so you will probably need to invest some of your own money. The more you can afford to invest yourself, the higher the chance of other people lending or investing, as they will see your own level of commitment to the business.
- **Credit cards**. Most people will throw up their hands in horror that I've included this option, but the millionaire entrepreneur Martin Webb, presenter of Channel 4's 'Risking It All', is living proof that you can start a business up using credit cards. This might be a useful option if you need a short amount of breathing space and you're sure you can start to sell quickly. It's not viable in the long term, though. If you can shop around for a 12-month 0 per cent interest deal, it gives you a bit of extra flexibility. But don't try to fund your whole venture this way.
- **Friends and family**. If you haven't got savings of your own, this is your next best bet. The advantages of borrowing from people you know are that you have even more incentive to make the business work but, at the same time, you may have a little more flexibility in terms of repayment arrangements. Do draw up a

proper repayment contract, though. On balance, it's probably better to borrow from family than from friends, however close they are. In my experience, family tend to be more understanding if things don't work out quite how you planned.

- **Grants**. Wouldn't it be wonderful if someone actually gave you some money to start up your business? Sounds like a dream, but there is actually a lot of grant money available for start-ups in the UK. The difficulty is accessing it and fighting your way through all the red tape. However, it's definitely worth contacting your local Business Link and/or local authority, especially if you're planning to operate in an area that has been singled out for regeneration or economic development support. If you're under 30, the Prince's Trust (www.princes-trust.org.uk) and the Shell LiveWire scheme (www.shell-livewire.org) are also worth checking out.

- **Banks**. Most people who are thinking of setting up a business and need funds to do so tend to think of the bank as their first port of call. But you need to look at things from the bank's perspective. Their primary purpose is not to be a funder of start-up businesses. They're not in the high-risk game. That doesn't mean it won't be possible to get funding from a bank, in the form of either an overdraft or a loan. But you'll need to have a very good business plan, preferably be able to show that you are putting a fair amount of investment into the business yourself, and be prepared to shop around. If you can't get a conventional loan because you have no assets to offer as security, you could investigate the Small Firms Loan Guarantee Scheme (SFLGS) run by the Department for Business, Enterprise and Regulatory Reform, which guarantees 75 per cent of the loan, thus significantly reducing the risk to the bank. You can find out more about the SFLGS at www.berr.gov.uk or www.businesslink.gov.uk. One word of warning, though: don't hold your breath. I've heard dozens of stories of people who meet the eligibility criteria still not being successful through the SFLGS, and it can be a red-tape minefield too.

- **Business angels**. A business angel is normally a wealthy person who is prepared to invest in a business for a relatively long-term return, probably because they have experience or a personal interest in particular business areas. Check out the British Business Angels' Association at www.bbaa.org.uk, or the service Angels' Den, www.angelsden.co.uk. For a fee of £99, you can post a business summary on a secure online database for business angels to view.

- **Venture capital**. It's actually pretty unlikely that you will get a venture capitalist to lend you money. That's because typically they are looking to invest sums above £2 million, and they will be looking for a relatively quick return for their money. Most business start-ups don't fall into this category.

You should explore every possible avenue of funding, armed with your business plan. Look on it as a learning experience too; take feedback on board and use it to keep refining your business idea.

Chapter 25

Marketing Your Business

The next two chapters focus on the two key elements of building your business: marketing and selling. Your marketing strategy is the way in which you make potential customers aware of your business; your sales strategy is the way in which you actually persuade them to buy. Each is as important as the other. If customers aren't aware of your services, clearly they can't buy them! Equally, it doesn't matter how many people know about what you do; if you can't persuade any of them to buy, you still don't have a business.

Marketing

If you've started to write your business plan, you'll already have given some thought to the best way to reach your target market. Let me repeat that your market *should* be targeted; customers want to feel that what you offer specifically meets their needs, so make sure that you have identified your niche and are clear about how your offering is tailored to your customers.

There is a huge range of ways in which you can market your business, and you'll probably want to use a mix of different approaches. The most effective tactics for your business will depend on what you are trying to sell, to whom and the best ways of reaching them. You'll also need to take account of your budget; it's all too easy to spend loads of money on expensive advertising and marketing campaigns, but see little return for your investment. Especially in the early days, my advice is to find the most cost-effective ways of raising awareness of your business, and that's what the advice in this chapter concentrates on. Be prepared for some trial and error. Some of the techniques you employ will work better than others, and you'll need to experiment a bit to see what works best for you.

Your website

Whatever your business, these days customers expect you to have a website. You don't have to spend a fortune on it, but it does need to be slick and professional. However technically competent you are, I recommend getting a professional to design your site. It will save you time, it needn't be too expensive – shop around for quotes from people who've designed sites you like – and it will look better. A website is a great way to introduce people to your business when you meet them: you can give them a very brief description of what you offer, and then invite them to have a look at your site. At the design stage, you do need to be very clear about what your website is for: is it intended simply to give customers more information about your services and encourage them to contact you, or will you be selling products via the site? The purpose of your site should inform its style, presentation and content, so make sure that your web designer is crystal clear about what you want the site to achieve. Above all, make sure that your site – like all of your marketing materials – contains a 'call to action'; after they have visited your site, what is the next thing you want people to do? For example, it might be to buy your product, or to contact you for more information or an initial consultation. Make it very clear what their next step should be, and make it easy for them to do it.

Here are some key website mistakes that small businesses make.

- A site that is too complicated. Whatever your web designer says, do not be tempted to go down the route of a flashy, complex site with lots of graphics, music and other gimmicks. Keep it simple; you want people to read the content, and most people's attention span on the web is pretty short. If your site takes too long to download, or they can't quickly find what they're looking for, they'll go somewhere else. And make sure the text and colours are easy on the eye. Finally, give the music a miss: you don't want to put off all those people who might be surfing the web at work!
- Not having a clear 'call to action'. I've said this before, but I can't repeat it too often: you must make it really clear what you want the person visiting your site to do next. Buy something? Call you?
- Not including a contact telephone number. You want people to be able to contact you straightaway, on impulse, not to have send you an email and then wait for your response. Of course, many people prefer to make contact by email in the first instance, so make sure both options are available.
- Not having a facility for online payment. If you are trying to sell products or services online, you must make it easy for people to buy then and there.
- Not including prices on your site. Some experts disagree with me here, and suggest that you shouldn't include prices because it encourages the potential customer to contact you to enquire about them. Frankly, I find it incredibly frustrating if I am looking at what someone is offering but can't easily see what it costs! So I would recommend transparent pricing, clearly set out on the site.
- Grammatical and spelling mistakes. You'd be surprised how many websites contain these, and how off-putting they are. If you can't be bothered to get the detail right when showcasing yourself and your work, think what that says to a potential customer about the quality of your service or product. As the saying goes, 'retail is detail'. Get it right.

Once you've got your site up and running, you need to maximise the chances of people finding it. Other marketing approaches (see below) will obviously have a big part to play here too, but what can you do online to raise your profile? Your website needs to be search-engine friendly. Try to choose a descriptive domain name, and include as many key words as you can in the content on the site. Don't wait for the search engines to find you, either; submit your URL details to as many as you can.

Research the online directories that are relevant to your business, and get yourself listed on those too. Some will be free, and some you will have to pay for, so use your discretion. Reciprocal links with other businesses can also improve your rankings and bring lots more visitors to your site. I deal with strategic alliances in more depth below, but the key is to think of other websites that are likely to attract a similar target market to yours, and seek to link up with them. If the services are genuinely complementary, so much the better. You can take this one step further by offering or participating in affiliate programmes, where other sites get commission for selling your product or service, and vice-versa.

Another good technique is to become a regular visitor and contributor to advice forums on other websites. You need to handle this carefully, as most sites specifically forbid direct marketing, but you can be a bit more subtle about it. For example, you could respond to someone else's query with some good advice, and include a brief reference to your business, or you could respond to them with advice and invite them to email you personally for more information. Just use your common sense and don't be too blatant.

It's probably worth experimenting with Google Adwords or other search engine advertising schemes, where you bid for key search terms and, depending on how much you bid compared with other providers, your website will be listed higher on the search engine. There are some downsides, though: firstly, visitors to your site will know that it is an Adwords listing, so they'll know you've paid for it rather than it naturally appearing at the top of the listing. Secondly, and probably more importantly, you pay per click through to your site, so it can be quite costly if your click-to-conversion rate is not high enough. And web users are lazy: even if they know the name of the site they want to visit, they'll often type it into a search engine rather than type in the domain name direct, so you could end up paying for people who already know you to visit your site. Again, it's a question of trial and error. Monitor your costs and sales carefully, to see if Adwords makes a worthwhile difference.

Once people have found your website, you need ways of making sure they keep coming back to it. I've read that people will visit a site anything between five and twelve times before they actually make a purchase. Of course, some people will buy straightaway, but if the majority of visitors to your site are just browsing and not yet ready to buy, you need to get them back to the site again and again. To use the jargon, you need to make your site 'sticky'. There are lots of ways you can do this. The key thing is to keep your site fresh. For example, you could publish weekly articles on topics relevant to your business, run a regular competition, offer free reports or other samples, or run an online advice forum (but be warned, this last option can be very time-consuming. You need to respond to queries promptly as well as monitor the appropriateness of other people's entries. And nothing looks worse than a forum that hasn't had anything posted on it for months.)

Most importantly, your aim is to capture visitors' email addresses so that you can keep in contact with them. You might do this by getting them to sign up to your regular newsletter. However, the last thing that most people want is yet more junk in their inbox, so make sure that your newsletter always offers something of value. That might be top tips, book reviews or special offers and discounts. Make it interesting enough for people to send on to friends and family, and you've got some nice viral marketing going on. Make sure that you send the newsletter out regularly. If you say it's weekly, then you need to send it out every week without fail. You might find it better to send out something really interesting fortnightly or even monthly, rather than end up scrabbling around every week to find something noteworthy to put in your newsletter.

A word of warning: maintaining a website can be enormously time-consuming. You can spend hours playing around with Google Adwords, website optimisation and tweaks to the site itself, none of which *guarantees* you more sales and can distract you from other kinds of marketing activity. So try to get the balance right. One book I read recently recommended spending two hours a day, five days a week on your site. That seems like a lot to me! But of course the time you devote to your site will depend on the part it plays in your marketing mix. If your service is completely web-based, then naturally you'll need to devote a lot of time and attention to it. But don't let it become a displacement activity for other forms of marketing that might be equally effective, but more daunting.

Finally, make sure that your website address is prominent on all your offline marketing material (see below), whether that's your business cards, flyers or press releases.

Bear in mind that while your website is the showcase for your business (or its platform, if you're selling online), it's only one part of your marketing strategy. At the time of writing, there are around 15 billion web pages, so the chances of people simply finding you are slim, to say the least. You're going to have to find ways of driving traffic to the site, so you will need other marketing approaches too.

Direct mail/flyers
Direct mail can be a very effective means of communicating with your target audience, but it can also be an immense waste of time and resources if it isn't done well. You need to get three things absolutely right: your message, your audience and your timing.

- **Message**. Every marketing book will tell you that a mail-shot (and any other promotional material, in fact) needs to follow a particular structure: AIDA (attention, interest, desire, action). In other words, you need to grab the customer's **attention** with a compelling headline, retain their **interest** by describing the benefits to them of what you offer, create in them a **desire** to take action, and make it very clear to them what that **action** should be (sign up for your workshop, visit your shop, etc). Offering a time-limited discount is a good way of encouraging them not just to take action, but to take action straightaway.

- **Audience**. Remember that you need to target your audience. If you are sending mail-shots, then you should do this by mailing your own contact database and/or relevant mailing lists. You can buy or rent the latter from list-brokering companies, or from large or specialist publishers. Bear in mind that renting or buying lists can be expensive, and will not necessarily give you access to your exact target market.
- **Timing**. This is the factor that can really affect your response rates (by the way, a good response rate for direct mail is about 1 to 2 per cent, so don't assume that if you've sent out 3,000 brochures, you're going to be inundated with enquiries. You won't be.) If you can time your promotion to fit with a particular seasonal need, you have a much better chance of people responding. Obvious examples include sending out mail-order catalogues before Christmas, or advertising your tax advisory services as the deadline for self-assessment looms.

Flyers can also be an excellent way of getting your message across, especially if your target market is geographically defined. For example, if you're opening a shop or restaurant, then giving out flyers promoting that fact in the local area, and/or doing leaflet drops, can reach a relevant audience relatively cheaply and easily. You can either deliver flyers yourself (or rope some friends in!), or arrange for them to be inserted into free community newspapers or the local evening paper. We have successfully marketed career-change workshops in the run-up to, and immediately after, Christmas and in the New Year by targeting commuters at London's main railway stations with leaflets advertising our seminars under a strapline like: 'Dreading going back to work in the New Year?', and offering an 'early bird discount' for pre-Christmas bookings.

Don't be afraid to target your competitors' customers, either. A few years ago a new tapas bar opened close to where I live. They got their first customers by standing outside the one existing tapas bar round the corner from them, which was always completely full and with a queue of customers, and offering those customers who were waiting an immediate table and a 10 per cent discount if they would only walk for a few minutes down the street. It worked a treat. Of course, they had to follow this up with food and service of just as high a quality as the original tapas bar, but they've done this and they're still thriving.

Advertising

I'll be honest here (not that I'm not always honest, of course) and say that, apart from a brief dalliance with Google Adwords, I have never spent a penny on advertising for my business. Why not? Simply because I believe that there are better and cheaper ways of contacting my target audience. That doesn't mean that advertising doesn't work, of course. But here, more than anywhere, is where you really need to be targeted. Think about it; you buy an expensive advertisement in a glossy magazine or national newspaper, and then you sit back and wait for the orders to roll in. Chances are, they don't. Why not? Look at it from the customer's perspective. Someone buys the magazine; they skim it and don't see your advertisement. They may even read it from cover to over and still not notice your advertisement. If they do notice it, it might not be relevant to them. Even if they notice it and it is relevant to them, they probably won't do anything about it straightaway, and then they misplace the magazine, or it gets put in the recycling pile you get the picture.

You might get a better response from advertising in a local newspaper, especially if your service is locally-based. But don't count on it. A life coach I know once spent £1,500 advertising a seminar in London's Evening Standard newspaper, paying £500 a day for three consecutive days, for a small black-and-white advertisement. On the day of the seminar, she asked every participant as they registered how they had heard about the workshop. Of the 50-something participants, only three had come along as a direct result of the newspaper advertisements. The rest had read about the workshop on her website. How much money did she make from the workshop? About £1,500. How much profit did she make? None.

I'm not saying that advertising won't work for your business – it depends to a large extent on the nature of the business - but I *am* saying that you need to be sure that what you are offering will be of interest to the majority of the publication's readership. It is probably more productive to think about putting an advertisement in the relevant supplement of a national or local newspaper, rather than its main body. Even better, focus on any trade press or publications specific to the industry or readership you are targeting. And be aware that one advertisement in isolation is unlikely to cut it; you'll need a series of them, and that's where the costs can really start to mount up.

Again, your message needs to be spot-on: a catchy headline, an interesting summary of the benefits of your product or service (including a case study, for example), and a call to action.

Finally, make sure you have a reliable method for monitoring the effectiveness of the advertisement: asking people who contact you as a result to quote a specific reference number, for example. That way at least you have some chance of measuring the cost-effectiveness of this approach for you and your business.

So far we've looked at the most common direct marketing techniques that businesses use. But there is also a range of indirect marketing approaches that, used well, can have an even greater impact on your sales.

Personal referrals

This is definitely one of the most effective marketing techniques. Getting other people to recommend your business probably has more weight than any marketing material you can devise. Ask your clients if they will provide a testimonial for your website, or if they would be prepared to tell their friends and colleagues about your service. Often clients would be very happy to recommend your service, but they just don't think to do it! So you do need to ask. Remember to follow up and say thank you when someone refers another potential client to you; it makes it much more likely that they'll think to do it again. You might even encourage (or thank) referrers by offering them a discounted rate on follow-up services, or some other gift that is appropriate to your product or service. I read about one guy who, when someone referred a client to him, sent them a wine glass as a thank-you gift, with a note saying 'This is the first in a set of six'. That's quite a nice incentive to send five more clients!

You can ask for professional as well as personal referrals; in other words, you ask other companies or businesses to recommend your product or service. If you can make this a reciprocal arrangement, so much the better, provided that you are genuinely happy to recommend the other party. There's another benefit in it for you, too: if you have a wide range of other businesses to which you can refer your clients, it positions you as a really useful source of knowledge, which in turn will drive people to refer others to you.

Of course, your ability to generate personal or professional referrals will be more limited in the early days, as you need to build up a client base to recommend you. But it's well worth being aware of this marketing tool from the outset, and asking your very first customers for referrals. If you have a mentor or support group then, as well as advising on your business, they can be a great source of referrals, especially if they hold a senior position or are well-connected.

Strategic alliances

Strategic alliances are really just a more formalised version of referrals. Teaming up with other businesses can be a great of way of increasing your exposure and making your offering available to a much wider audience. The trick is to identify other companies or businesses who are marketing to the same target audience as you, but with a different product or service. You then team up with them to promote each others' services, for example through your website or a joint campaign. You might even offer your service or product to their clients at a discounted rate, which provides extra custom for you and added value for them. For example, a health club might be prepared to promote your life-coaching services in return for a discounted rate for their members. People who are interested in their health and wellbeing might also be in the market for coaching, so it's a good targeted approach.

You can take this one step further by actually collaborating on projects together. For example, I regularly run workshops in conjunction with one of my strategic alliance partners, Sue from QC Image Consultancy. Targeted at young professionals, the workshop covers career change and advancement (my bit), and how to dress professionally (Sue's bit). Because the workshop covers a wider range of subject matter than one I could run on my own, we get a better response rate. Yes, of course I have to split the income with Sue, but we have more of it because we have more attendees, and we also have a higher chance of follow-up business. Last but not least, the two of us have great fun!

You do need to be confident in the quality of the service offered by anyone you're thinking of entering into an alliance with (and they in you, of course). You don't want your own fledgling reputation to be damaged by poor customer service from someone whom you've recommended.

By the way, don't discount the possibility of entering into a strategic alliance with a competitor. This might seem a bit counter-intuitive: why on earth would you work with someone you're in competition with? But it can be a good approach for small businesses because it can help them to access contracts and customers that they otherwise wouldn't. Two small businesses working in collaboration can often punch above their weight, and make a more credible pitch than one small business on its own. Why? Because together they have more expertise, more resources and more capacity and capability. For example, small businesses bidding for (lucrative!) public sector contracts are often at a disadvantage because big players in the market will also be bidding. Collaborating with a competitor could help a small business get in on the action. You don't need to share all your business secrets with your competitor, you just need to bring what you can to the particular project you're collaborating on.

Finally, consider the possibility of piggy-backing. This is where you get someone who is much more famous than you are to endorse your product or service. Think about the people who are experts or celebrities in your industry, or a complementary field. How could you entice them to support or promote your business? The secrets to doing this successfully are: make sure what you're offering is top-quality (which should go without saying, in any case); be 100 per cent professional in your approach (again, that should go without saying); and don't be afraid to ask! After all, the worst they can do is say 'no', and when it comes to selling (see below), you're going to get used to hearing that word anyway.

Networking

We've already seen the value of networking for those who are job-hunting, and it's a very useful tool for those are who trying to build their business, too. It can be a source of new business leads, a way of building your own expertise, meeting experts in other areas like HR or finance, or simply a great way to meet like-minded people and get some moral support. The networking groups that will be most useful for you will depend on what you want to get from the experience, so be as clear about that as you can. Whatever your goals, make sure that you can talk positively and succinctly about your business.

You can take networking one step further by offering to be a contributor to, rather than just a participant at, a networking event or workshop. This is a good way of raising your profile and building your credibility as an expert in your field. Even if your audience is not directly in the market for your products or services, each of them will know lots of people who might be. And it's an opportunity to ask for feedback on what you're doing, and to get some good testimonials that you can put on your website. Check out your library or local newspaper for information about business and community groups in your area who might be interested to hear what you are doing.

As well as face-to-face networking, there's a wide range of online networking resources that you might well find helpful for advice on your business, or for building up business leads. Two of the best-known are Ecademy and Linked-In, and clients of mine have reported good results from using these. As with anything else, you get out what you put in, so there's a time commitment to making online networking work for you. As ever, a bit of trial and error is probably needed.

The new online phenomenon, of course, is the social networking site: MySpace, Facebook and so on. I think that social networking could be one of the big marketing tools of the future. Think about it: the best way of marketing your business is to get other people to do it for you – word-of-mouth referrals. By tapping into your social network, you can leverage all the people who already know and trust you. But a word of warning: you can't use this medium for heavy direct marketing. Rather, you need to build up your reputation as an expert or guru in your field: someone to whom people will turn for the advice they need. Your aim should be to become a trusted part of the online community, whether it's a social networking site or an online forum for specific business issues.

Business cards

When you're networking and meeting people in other ways, you'll want to give them a copy of your business card. One quick tip here: make sure that you make the most of your card. Why leave the back of it blank, for example? You could include a simple call to action: a 10 per cent discount on your offering, or the information that by visiting your website the person can download a free report. And make sure you always have plenty of your cards with you; you never know whom you might meet and when. Think imaginatively about where you might place your cards, too: local libraries, shops, restaurants or health clubs might have noticeboards where you can advertise. Take every free opportunity that you can to promote your services.

PR (public relations)

There's an air of mystery around PR, and many small business owners start to feel nervous when you mention the words 'journalist' or 'media'. But put simply, PR is about engaging the public with your business through positive media coverage. Getting your business featured in local and national media is a great way to boost awareness of your services, as well as your credibility. And it doesn't cost you anything except your time. Be warned, though: PR is usually a long-term game, not a quick hit. Just because you get a mention in the local newspaper, don't expect the phone to start ringing off the hook. Probably only a small proportion of people who buy the paper will see the piece, let alone read it or contact you as a result. But regular mentions in the media will help to build your profile over time, and can be very useful in persuading potential customers of your status or expertise.

So how do you go about getting good media coverage? The first thing is to be proactive; there's no point in sitting around waiting for journalists to find you, because they probably won't. (That said, it is well worth registering with a website that links the media with experts, allowing journalists to search the database for people who are knowledgeable on the area they are writing about. I've had a lot of exposure via www.expertsources.com). Secondly, you need to be clear about what your PR goals are. Yes, you want to get positive publicity, but what precisely is the message you want to get across? Be specific. Think about the hooks you can use for your message. What's hot in the news right now? What current trends are relevant to what you're doing? What can you contribute to the debate?

Then you need to think about your target audience (again). Who are you trying to reach, and which media are the best ways of reaching them? Think about what your customers are likely to read or listen to, which websites or online communities they are likely to frequent, and so on. Draw up a list of relevant publications, which can be a mixture of national, local and specialist press. It's also worth checking out your local radio stations; have a look at their schedule and figure out which shows are most likely to be interested in your product or service.

When it comes to writing a press release, the key is to get people curious. Kick it off with a punchy headline, and summarise the point you are making in the first paragraph. Try to make your release relevant to something that is current in the news or the industry you are targeting. Journalists receive hundreds of press releases every day, and if they don't immediately see the relevance of yours it will go straight in the bin. If you can, include a short case study or testimonial; human interest angles are always good. More detailed information about you and your service or product can be included in a factual 'Notes to editors' section at the end of the release. Keep the whole thing to one side of A4 if you possibly can, and make sure you include your contact details!

Another good tip is to include freelancers in your distribution list. Because they only get paid when one of their articles is printed, it's obviously in their interest to get the piece published, and they will often tout it round a number of publications in an attempt to do so, doing a lot of the hard work for you!

Always, always treat journalists with great respect. They are busy people (yes, I know, aren't we all, but journalists have to be much more deadline-focused than most of us). If a journalist contacts you, treat it as top priority; if you don't get back to them pretty much straightaway, they'll move on to another contact and you'll have missed your opportunity. And if that happens more than once, you'll disappear from their radar completely. Journalists want contacts who are reliable, readily available and who always come up with the goods.

Finally, remember that in PR you will win some and lose some. Sometimes your competitor will get a mention rather than you. Don't fret about it. If you are consistent and persistent in your approach, over time you will get coverage that will help to build up your reputation and your brand.

Check out www.doyourownpr.com for some great advice and tips on how to run your own successful PR campaign.

Get published

One of the best ways of establishing yourself as an expert in your area is to get yourself published. Whether you're selling a product or service, think about how you can add value by writing about what you know. That doesn't have to mean writing a whole book, which can be great for your credibility but is extremely time-consuming. It could be something as simple as a list of 'top tips' on your website, which you can submit to other relevant websites or publications. Websites in particular are always looking for new content to keep them fresh, so check out the key sites in your industry sector and see if you can submit material to them. You could also consider writing a series of short e-books that people can download from your site; you could offer some for free and charge a small fee for others, which has the benefit of bringing you in some 'passive' income. And once you've written it, you can sell it over and over again.

Your marketing materials

Whichever of the above elements make up your marketing strategy, you need to focus on the benefits of your product or service, not just its features. In other words, what does it do for the customer? Your marketing material should be focused on the customer, not you. If you're planning to print brochures for direct mail, or to set up a website, it's a good idea to spend a little money getting a professional copywriter to give your content the once-over. They will be experienced in drafting copy and headlines that attract customers' attention. You will, though, need to make sure that they understand fully what you are offering and why it is different, so that they can hit the right buttons with their copy. Again, get as much feedback as you can from customers themselves (or potential customers) about your marketing materials. What attracted them? What were the phrases that caught their attention and pulled them in? In the early days, you can test out your marketing materials on focus groups of friends and colleagues, or even on passers-by if you have the nerve! Remember that the most important thing is what attracts the customer, not what you *think* will attract the customer.

Finally – and this is probably the most useful tip of all – think about how you can offer outstanding value upfront. A great way of getting potential customers' attention is to offer them something for free. Again, that could be top tips in your area of expertise, or a free sample of your product. This isn't about undermining your business, it's about building your reputation as a trusted expert to whom people will turn when they need more help or information, which they're more likely to be willing to pay for if you have already demonstrated your ability to help them.

However good your marketing strategy is, and however many potential customers you reach, you'll only make money if you can persuade people actually to buy. The next chapter looks at how to sell effectively.

Chapter 26

Getting People to Buy

Your marketing strategies are bringing people to your website, or your door. But how do you persuade them to part with their precious cash? The idea of selling makes most entrepreneurs panic, so here are some thoughts to comfort you at the outset.

- **Rejection is a part of the process**. Be prepared for lots of it. We don't like selling because we don't like the thought of rejection, of people saying 'no' to us. But it's going to happen, and the sooner you get used to that idea, the better. The trick is not to take it personally, even though it *feels* personal. At the end of the day, people aren't actually rejecting *you*, they just don't need – or think they need – what you have to offer.

- **Often, it's about timing**. Most sales come from approaching the right person at the right time. There's nothing more scientific to it than that. Yes, you need to have a great offering and be able to show the benefits to your potential customer and why it's better than your competitors' product, but if the timing isn't right for the customer, they won't buy. The good news is that there are things you can do to improve your chances of a sale, by getting the timing right (or at least better). Think about when there is likely to be the greatest demand for your product or service. And think about the business cycles of your potential customers. For example, public sector organisations often operate on an annual budgeting cycle, which means that if they don't spend their budget by the end of the financial year, they can't carry it over into the following one. So if you are trying to sell to the public sector, whether it's training courses or IT support, January to March can be a good time to contact them.

- **Persistence pays off**. You'll most likely need to make several contacts with a prospect before they are ready to buy, so you will need to be persistent. But that's not the same as being a pain. You don't want people to refuse to take your calls! Remember that persistence is not just about chasing one particular sale; it's about asking *enough* people, as well as asking often enough.

- **The best thing to do is just get started**. Set yourself a target for the number of calls you want to make in a day or a week, and just get on with it. If you're really holding back from sending that email or picking up the phone, look back to the tips for handling procrastination in Chapter 19. In particular, don't be afraid to bribe yourself! So if you make your target number of calls, you can count yourself finished for the day, or treat yourself to a nice cappuccino or a trip to the local bookshop: whatever will motivate you to get the job done.

Identifying sales targets

Your marketing strategy should have helped you to identify your most likely customers – your target market. These are the people with whom you need to make proactive contact. It's not enough to hope that they see your website/brochure/advertisement and take action on it. Even if someone is interested in what you have to offer, all the other demands on their time are likely to mean that they just never get around to contacting you.

The easiest place to start is with people who already know and trust you, or who can recommend you to others. As we've seen already, a personal referral is the best way of opening doors. So think about everyone you know who might be able to help you make the contacts you need, even if they themselves are not in the market for your service.

Another effective sales target is the customers that you already have. Think of ways in which you can sell additional products or services to existing customers. It's much easier to sell to an existing customer than a new one; they already know and trust you, and you have a good idea of what their needs and preferences are. So think creatively about other offerings that might appeal to them. Keep in touch with them regularly (not just when you want to sell them something new), and keep giving them value through newsletters and top tips, or simply something like emailing them an article you came across that you thought might interest them. Let them know you care and are thinking about them. This 'customer maintenance' sounds time-consuming, and it is, but it's a lot less time-consuming than trying to source new customers from scratch.

Of course, there will come a point when you've exhausted all your existing contacts and leads. That's when you need to venture out into the scary world of cold-calling. You simply have to do this: you absolutely can't leave it to luck and hope that your big break will just happen to come your way. It won't. But selling doesn't have to be as terrifying as you might think.

The sales process

The selling process has three main stages: getting your opening, making your pitch, and closing the sale.

● **Getting your opening**. The first thing you need to do when you are cold-calling is identify the right person to speak to. You have to find the person with the authority to make the purchasing decision for your particular offering. This is more easily said than done, but the effort will pay off. The more clearly and succinctly you can describe exactly what you are offering and whom in the organisation it is most likely to benefit, the better. Once you know the person you need to connect with, I have found that it is often easier to make the initial contact by email. If you're calling 'cold', especially to someone senior in the company, your chances of getting put through are low, and the chances of their calling you back are even lower. But if you email them, there's more likelihood that they will read your email and, if you can keep it short, punchy and to the point, there's more chance of their responding. It's also much less scary to send an email! At this stage, you're not trying to sell them anything; you're simply asking for a brief meeting to discuss whether your product or service might be of value to them. If you don't get a response to your email within, say, a week, then follow up with a phone call; the fact that you have emailed them at least gives you a hook for your conversation. When you call, my advice is to introduce yourself and summarise briefly what you wrote in your email, then ask if you can book a time to meet them, or at least call them for a slightly longer chat. That way you are less likely to get fobbed off with the line 'I'm too busy to talk now'. You also have the opportunity to prepare fully for a meeting or call that will actually take place, rather than psyching yourself up for a pitch that you don't get the opportunity to make.

- **Making your pitch**. In an ideal situation, the person you are trying to sell to will agree to a short meeting. It's much easier to make an effective pitch face-to-face than over the telephone. However, there will be occasions, either because of the other person's time constraints or because of their location, when a phone call is your only option. Either way, the key things to remember are: try to identify with the customer on a personal level and build up rapport (without being smarmy!); ask questions and be ready to show how your service meets the customer's needs; and try to offer great value upfront. For example, if you are trying to sell training courses, why not offer to send through the notes from some courses you have already designed or run, to give an idea of their content, or even offer to run one workshop for free? Often, of course, customers will come up with a range of objections as to why they can't buy your service. Learn to look on objections as a good thing. Yes, really; they mean that the customer is thinking seriously about your offer. There are three main objections that you will encounter: 'I don't need it', 'I already have a supplier', and 'I can't afford it'. The best response to the first of these is not to be too pushy, but to explain again the benefits of what you offer and how you see it helping them. In response to the second, don't be tempted to criticise their existing supplier, but explain how you are different and perhaps offer a free trial if that's appropriate. If the customer says they can't afford your service, explain the value that you can add or the money you can save them in the longer term and, again, consider offering an initial free or discounted service.

- **Closing the sale**. If your pitch has been a good one, and you have focused on identifying and responding to the potential customer's needs, and answering their objections, this is not as difficult as you might think. A simple tactic is: just ask for the business! Often the direct approach is the best one. A quick tip here; once you've asked the question about whether the customer would like to buy, *keep quiet*. Waffling on and repeating yourself about the benefits of what you're offering only makes you look desperate and distracts the customer. Give them a minute to think about it and don't be tempted to jump in with more conversation while they do. You'll find that the customer themselves will break the silence, often by saying 'yes'. And if they don't, at least you leave or finish the call with your dignity intact. If you really don't feel comfortable with asking for the sale outright, another good approach is the 'alternative' method. So, if you're trying to persuade a company to buy your training workshops, for example, you could say: 'Would you prefer the stress management course or the negotiating skills course?' The hidden assumption is that they're going to choose one of them, but you are letting them retain the power in the negotiation because they get to make the choice. Similarly, you could offer options with different cost implications: 'Would you prefer a half-day course or a full day?'

Most of the advice above applies in particular where you are trying to sell to a company or organisation. Where you are trying to sell to individuals, your approach will be more dependent on their contacting you as a result of your marketing efforts. That said, make sure that you're not missing a trick: just because your product or service is aimed at individuals doesn't mean that there isn't a corporate market for it too. Many employers are increasingly looking to find new and interesting ways of rewarding or motivating their staff, so do think about how you might market to individuals through their workplace.

Remember, you don't have to be a sales professional to be successful. You just need to have a great product or service that you really believe in, a fairly thick skin to deal with objections and rejection, and always, always to keep your customers' wants and needs at the forefront of your mind.

Some Final Thoughts

I want to use this final chapter to highlight some of the most important issues to think about in terms of your career and your life. If you take nothing else from this book, at least take some time to focus on the ideas below.

Your work is not your life

This might seem like an odd way to end a book on career development. After all, hasn't the whole focus of this book been on how to work better, be more effective, make a bigger impact and be more successful? Well, yes, but that's not the whole picture. Because the secret to success is being satisfied in every part of your life, not just your work. That's why I want to conclude by encouraging you to think about your life and lifestyle as a whole, and not just your work in isolation. Work is something that should add to, rather than detract from, the rest of your life. But it's not your whole life, and it shouldn't be. Keep it in perspective.

Remember, again, the saying that no one ever lay on their deathbed wishing they'd spent more time in the office. It's true. Fulfilling, meaningful work that gives us a real buzz and a sense of satisfaction is an important part of our lives, but it's only that: a part. The chances are that the real fun, excitement and happiness in our lives come mainly from how we spend our time outside of work, and that's how it should be. If you spend all your time working, or thinking about work, you're missing out on everything else. It's not a good way to live.

Get the balance right

The phrase 'work–life balance' is one that is bandied around a lot these days. In many ways that's a good thing; it shows that more of us, and more employers, are recognising that you don't have to sell your soul to the corporate devil to be successful, and that people actually work better when their work is not all-consuming. But the important thing to remember is that there's no one, perfect definition of what constitutes a good work–life balance. It depends on what your personal priorities are, and it also depends to some extent on the stage you are at in your career. If you are in your twenties and thirties, trying to climb the corporate ladder and build a reputation for yourself, there will be times when work just has to come first, when you're working long hours and giving it everything you've got. And as long as that's part of your strategy to get to where you want to be, and not just a displacement activity so that you can ignore other areas of your life, that's fine. But you need to make sure that you are happy in all those other areas of your life too. If you're not, your professional success will feel pretty empty.

Look at the big picture

If you want to have the life you desire, you need to be clear about your values, know what your priorities are, and make sure that the way in which you allocate your time reflects both your values and your priorities. It's that simple.

Go back to the values exercises in Chapter 2. Look at how you rated each of the categories of your life: physical environment, health, finances, friends and family, partner, fun and recreation, and of course your career. Remember the question that I asked you to ask yourself: 'What changes do I need to make so that I am living in accordance with my values?' If you haven't completed that exercise, do it now. Not just the career section, but all the other parts too. So, if one of your values is financial security, for example, what changes do you need to make in your career, your leisure time or your relationships to put yourself in a position where you can start to save rather than just spend? Or if having a really close relationship with your partner is your priority, what changes do you need to make to how you spend your time?

Your exercise has probably thrown up lots of areas in which you could do with making changes. I don't expect you to tackle them all at once. What you should do is put them in order of priority and importance. In which areas would making a change really matter?

Make time for your life

Make sure that you are spending your time in a way that reflects your values and priorities. It's one thing to decide what your priorities are, but nothing's going to change until you start to allocate your time in accordance with your priorities. Undertake a time audit. For a week or so, keep a diary of how you actually spend your time. Does it reflect your priorities? Does it *really*? Be honest with yourself. How much of your spare time do you spend watching rubbish on television? It might not be rubbish that you're watching, but it's still not the best use of your time. For example, how much time do you spend watching cookery programmes while you eat a microwave meal? Why not get into the kitchen and actually cook something? Perhaps one of your priorities is learning. But how much time do you really devote to that? What do you read and how much time do you spend reading? I read a shocking statistic the other day: 60 per cent of US adults don't read a single book after leaving high school. I'll bet the figure for the UK isn't too different. How can you learn, develop and expand your horizons if you never read anything?

It's easy to get into the habit of saying 'I don't have time for x', but the truth is that you have the same amount of time as everyone else. It's how you use it that makes the difference. So get a grip: if you think you don't have time to do the things that you say are important, look at all the ways in which you waste your time. Dump some of the rubbish and start to focus on doing the things that will effect real change.

One of the most constructive things you can do is to make more time for yourself by learning to say 'no'. How many times have you agreed to go to a party, or a function, or meet up with friends when you didn't really want to, but it was easier to agree than to say no? Start getting into the habit of putting yourself first for a change. When I say this to clients, they often respond that they don't want to be 'selfish'. But you *have* to be selfish: the only person who will ever put you first is you. If you spend your time with people who drain you, or doing things that you don't enjoy doing, you simply end up frustrated, resentful and emotionally depleted. And that's not a person who is much fun to be around! So the best thing you can do for other people is to put yourself at the top of your priority list. That might mean scheduling time in your diary to do things that make you feel good: going for a walk, having a long bath, relaxing with a good book and a glass of wine. Or it might mean ditching some of the stuff that takes up time and that you get no pleasure out of: housework, or 'friends' who moan all the time, for example. Ditch the friends, get a cleaner, do whatever you need to so that you have time in your diary just for you. Trust me, the people around you will thank you for it because you'll be so much easier to live with!

Make the change

Finally, the most important point of all: the only person who can make the changes you need to make is *you*. Nothing's going to change if you don't take action. If you want to change your career or get that promotion, you have to get out there and actually do something about it. Reading this book (or any other), even going to see a career coach, are good starting points but they're not enough. You need to take real action. If you want to improve your finances, or your relationship, or your health, you not only need to have a plan, you need to put it into action. You need to make things happen. And the only way to do that is to start doing what you need to do.

Thinking about the changes you want to make isn't enough. Knowing what you need to do isn't enough. Even having a plan isn't enough. The only thing which will make a difference to your career or any other aspect of your life is action.

Enough said. Put this book down now and go and do one thing that will make a difference to your life. And then keep going!

Good luck. And if I can help you at all in any way, please drop me an email at jenny@citylifecoaching.com. I'd love to hear from you.

Case Studies

Throughout this book, we've looked at a range of ways in which you can manage your career other than the traditional nine-to-five model. In this chapter, some people who've done just that tell their stories in their own words. Some of them have been clients of mine, others are people I've met along the way, but all of their experiences are interesting, inspiring and unique.

Richard Fanshawe
From investment banking to adventure sports with a few stops on the way

I used to be an investment banker in London, living with my brother and some good university friends. Shame I didn't see them very much! My brother and I would sometimes meet in the street or in our kitchen in the early hours of the morning having just finished work, but more often, we would go for entire weeks without seeing each other.

Just before I completed my third year, I was allocated to a project that finished me off. I felt ill, totally demoralised, stuck in a rut and tired of life, at the grand old age of 23! It didn't bode well for my future.

A combination of several factors influenced my decision to take time out in search of what I really wanted: a lifestyle and work that was more my style.

- I couldn't stand the work I was doing. I had been sucked into it for all the wrong reasons: principally money, glamour and my failure more fully to investigate career options after university other than the 'big three' (banking, consultancy and accountancy).
- I hated the total unpredictability of my working hours.
- I hated never being able to make plans for fear of having to cancel, and having next to no control over my own life.
- I loved my hobbies – especially travelling – and couldn't stand not having the time or the energy left to pursue them.
- I was diagnosed with a kidney defect that required eight hours of surgery and a painful four-month recuperation period.
- A friend who was trying to make his name as a freelance journalist in Iraq was murdered in Baghdad in a taxi queue. More than anything else, this taught me that life is very unpredictable, very precious and that you should make the most of every opportunity before it is too late.

So I resigned, with the full intention of getting my operation over and done with, getting well again and then doing all the things I'd longed to do, but thought better of at the time. This included:

- pursuing my passion for outdoor sports, in particular skiing and watersports, which I had unwillingly been neglecting;
- learning Spanish; and
- travelling further afield to broaden my horizons, see some more of the world and meet some new people.

So, I went on a course in Argentina and qualified as a ski instructor. I went sailing around Croatia, Italy, Sicily, Malta and finally arrived in Tunisia. I worked in Sunshine Village in Banff (in the Canadian Rockies), teaching skiing for a season, which is where I met my current business partner. We both then enrolled in a Spanish language school for four months in Tarifa in southern Spain, learning Spanish in the morning and kitesurfing during the afternoons.

During this time, we adapted an existing business idea to involve the courses we had just undertaken. We both qualified as IKO (International Kiteboarding Organisation) kitesurf instructors and worked in Tarifa for a further two years, making contacts, gaining industry experience, refining our business plan and selecting the best partner businesses to make our business, Fluid Feeling, a reality. Fluid Feeling is an adventure-sports travel business focused on career break and time-out courses and holidays in some of the most amazing locations.

Our aim is to provide the kind of career break and time-out courses that we were looking for when we took our breaks. In addition to fun, relaxation and exhilaration, we want to add an often-overlooked component: guidance as to how best to make use of your time off and how to think constructively about your future. The business has been a real eye-opener and one hell of a challenge to get off the ground. But the beauty about this kind of business is that there is no typical day. We will do everything from admin and accounts, right through to hosting the courses and washing boards and kites at the end of a day's instructing. The combination of office and outdoor work (especially on the beach!) is a very satisfying one, and in the gaps in-between we still find some time to go kiting or surfing ourselves.

This whole process has taken the best part of four years. I set off with clear ideas of what I wanted to do, but with little guidance as to future careers and clear end objectives. All that I knew was that I was looking for a better way of life, more satisfying for me, based on my passions, interests and abilities. I prefer variety to routine, I wanted to be my own boss, I enjoy the business aspects but I also love my company's chosen sports. Despite the highly competitive nature of our industry, I believe that our genuine interest in what we do reflects in the service and products we provide.

Check out Richard's website at www.fluidfeeling.com.

Debbie Davidson
Combining acting and business consulting

For someone who has always known what she wanted to do, my career has been extremely varied. A few years back I believe I was often defined (by others) as a jack of all trades but master of none, but now I am seen as someone with a portfolio career. I work as a professional actress, and am also the director of a successful consulting firm. For someone who needs diversity and stimulation, this career structure ticks all the boxes.

Looking back, I realise I spent lots of time and energy trying to define what I should be, dabbling in both the arts and the business world, wondering which one fulfilled me the most. After a lengthy trial-and-error process, I finally admitted to myself that neither in their own right provided the satisfaction I needed, and so I toyed with the idea of combining the two.

People often think the art–business mix is an unusual one; however, I believe my success in both is due to understanding the complementary factors. My business knowledge often gives me the edge when finding acting work, and my artistic bent helps me find creative solutions in the business. Business processes and marketing initiatives work well in an artistic life, and I find myself savvier about the industry than many other actors out there. The business benefits from having a director who is not completely absorbed by it and can retain perspective.

My biggest challenge is time, and it is important to know what the priorities are on any given day. I keep the diary flexible, delegate where I can and make sure I structure in a life. It's never a 50/50 split, as both careers grow at different rates. It can often feel like spinning plates, but that's the beauty of a portfolio career. To be honest, I wouldn't have it any other way.

James Uffindell
Serial entrepreneur, founder of Oxbridge Applications, Pure Potential and Bright London

I'm of the persuasion that whilst entrepreneurs are born and not made, the environment one grows up in can shape any pre-existing entrepreneurial disposition. Being exposed to a self-employed father helped me to develop commercial awareness, and going to university developed my ability to think strategically, come up with independent and creative ideas and analyse their economic validity.

I started my first business, Oxbridge Applications, in my last year at Oxford in 1999. I identified that there was a significant problem with bright students not being adequately prepared for their Oxbridge interviews. To me it was obvious that some kind of service was needed to help these students (and their parents and schools) through the application process. I marketed the business by identifying my key audience and where it could be reached (open days, PR in broadsheet newspapers and schools). The business was funded initially by my student loan, then organic cash-flow. Oxbridge Applications has now helped over 30,000 students apply to Oxbridge and has a success rate of twice the average, working with around 10 per cent of all applicants every year.

Realising there was a major problem with bright state school students not applying to Britain's best universities, I then co-founded Pure Potential to help 10,000 students a year and for free. Pure Potential is funded by 50 leading graduate recruiters (including Goldman Sachs, PwC and Clifford Chance).

Bright London, which launched in April 2008, is a revolutionary careers service to help bright graduates, for free, with their career choices. I just got too frustrated seeing bright people leave good universities and not benefit from adequate support in the first five years of their career.

Looking back over the seven years since I left university, it amazes me that my businesses are flourishing; when I started I had no business experience, no contacts and only a tiny amount of capital. I would give the following advice to anyone starting up on their own.

- **Minimise the downside**. Of course you expect your idea to succeed, but remember that 90 per cent of businesses go bust in the first year. Make sure that if things don't go to plan you can keep on trading; this means being careful with lavish overheads you would like, but don't really need. Hope for the best, plan for the worst.
- **Be ruthless**. You're not running a charity. Don't be afraid of getting the best deal in all of your transactions and selling to your customers for a price that accurately reflects the value of your product. Price is all too often a tiny part of a decision as to whether a client will buy or not; don't be shy of getting what you're worth.
- **People**. Your staff are the most important part of your business: you have to interact with them every day, they represent you to your clients and they generate ideas. Take time to make sure you find the best people and you clearly communicate your vision to them.
- **Identify your skills and avoid diversification**. I firmly believe you should find the thing you're good at and stick to it; for me it's events that help people fulfil their potential, and this applies to all three of my businesses. Too often entrepreneurs stumble because they can't see one idea through to the end, and they start other unrelated concepts. Stick to the knitting! Get the core right and the rest will follow; anything built on shaky foundations won't last.

www.oxbridgeapplications.com, www.purepotential.org, www.brightlondon.com.

Kate Harrison
From television producer to successful author
I always loved writing, but 'author' never appeared in the school careers handbooks, so I decided to become a journalist instead. It was fascinating, but

also seriously unfriendly in terms of work–life balance, with irregular hours and constant deadlines. I worked for the BBC as a reporter and producer for more than a decade, but the writing bug never disappeared. I'd write short stories on holiday, but didn't have time for more than that.

Then, over Christmas 2001, I finally had an idea for a novel, *Old School Ties*, and wrote furiously. By June 2002 I had a finished manuscript, an agent and a publisher; every writer's dream come true. Alas the advance wasn't going to keep me in the style to which I'd become accustomed, so there was no giving up the day job. I wasn't alone; the average published writer makes just £7,000 a year, with no sick leave, no holidays and no guarantees past the current contract. But getting the deal gave me the confidence to plan for a future in which I could swap journalism for full-time novel-writing.

I found a (rare) TV job that allowed me to work four days a week, and crammed the novel-writing into the other day and evenings/weekends. I also decided, on my agent's advice, to move publishers after that first book; this was quite a gamble, when I had no guarantees that I'd find another publisher! That was probably the scariest moment, but it was worth it financially; the advance for the second book looked more like something I could live off.

It took me more than four years from having that first book idea to working out that I could afford to take redundancy and become a 'proper' author. In June 2006 I joined the ranks of the self-employed.

I still say yes to running occasional courses in TV and writing (including one in China!), partly for the extra income but mainly because it's a nice change from the solitary work of writing novels. I love the freedom, but I'm pretty disciplined. My fifth book, *The Secret Shopper's Revenge*, is out in a few months, but there's no resting on my laurels: I've already started my seventh.

Even though my books have been bought by publishers in the US, Germany and Russia, freelance life can still seem precarious, but I feel so lucky to be one of those people who has realised their childhood dream, even if it did take me a while to get there.

www.kate-harrison.com

Louise Bloor
From politics to perfume and law

After leaving university I worked as a researcher for an MP. It is a demanding job, with hundreds of letters to be answered every week, a packed diary to manage and a pressing parliamentary timetable, and I learnt an enormous amount in short amount of time.

After about five years I felt I wanted a new challenge and would like to work for myself. I have always been interested in perfume and so I began to explore that area, visiting perfume houses and reading books on the subject. I contacted the author of one, a bespoke perfumer in California, and she agreed to tutor me.

After two years studying and practising in my spare time I launched Louise Bloor Limited, a perfume company that specialises in creating a one-off perfume for each individual client.

As with starting work in Westminster, this new challenge taught me a lot in a short space of time. Doing everything yourself means you really learn what works and what doesn't. I had to learn skills such as marketing, accounting and product development. I developed a large client base and also a corporate events service, organising events at which clients are treated to their own bespoke perfume.

However, I missed working with other people and after much reflection decided to retrain as a lawyer, something I had considered when I first graduated. I studied full-time for a law conversion course and funded it by working two days a week at Westminster and fulfilling perfume orders. The course is very demanding and I have never worked so hard in my life. But I loved studying the law and am looking forward to qualifying in the summer and to a new job as a barrister for the government.

Although it has been hard work I feel very fortunate to have been able to explore different careers and to find what really suits me.

www.louisebloor.com

Paula Gardner
From hands-on to online

I started my own PR company back in 1991. I was 21 years old, and although I hadn't worked in the corporate market for long I knew that being my own boss was the only way that I wanted to work. And I loved it. I loved being able to take the morning off and go swimming, or meet someone for a long leisurely lunch. My clients were in the music industry, just because that's where I had previously worked. But it's an industry full of big egos and small pockets, so I soon switched to hospitality, which was much more lucrative, and eating out at places like L'Escargot was a pretty nice perk. The great thing about PR is that you can do a lot of it in the evenings or weekends and go out and have fun when everyone else is at work, which I have to admit I did get a kick out of!

But by the time 2002 came around I'd had three children and found that traditional PR wasn't working as well for me. The restaurant industry was changing from being lots of small independents to larger groups or corporates. Added to that, ongoing clients often feel that they are entitled to call you at all hours of the day or night, and my previous PR speciality of gorgeous hotels and restaurants wasn't quite so easy with three children to juggle. I took on wealth coach Nicola Cairncross as one of my clients and it was through working with her that I came up with the idea of Do Your Own PR, where people can buy courses that take them through how to plan and implement a PR campaign for their business. The beauty of it was that it was online (no expensive childcare and meetings miles away for me) and much of it is passive; it's great coming home to find an order in my inbox. I also work with a large number of clients from different industries, and I relish the variety.

I've always been a great believer in living by your wits. I want my children to have a number of skills and certain amount of business acumen so they don't feel as though they are being thrust on one road for the rest of their lives, and that they have a number of resources they can rely upon.

www.doyourownpr.com

Selina Barker
Freestyler

I always knew I wasn't going to follow the conventional nine-to-five, five-days-a-week job, in front of the same computer in the same office day after day, year after year. Some people love routine and structure, and enjoy the security of each day being predictable, as well as knowing exactly where the next pay cheque is going to come from. I'm not one of those people; I never have been, and it didn't take me long to realise it wasn't something I was going to learn to love.

Some people might see my approach to work as the haphazard behaviour of a person lost and not knowing what else to do. On the contrary, I know exactly what I'm doing; I'm confident, in control and loving every day of work that I do. I have a lot of strings to my bow and being able to play all of them is a true gift I give to myself. It gives me a quality of life, sense of freedom and opportunity for new experiences that I never thought was possible. No one told us at school that you could be this creative with your career.

I didn't set out to create a portfolio career; I'd never even heard of the term. It began as a trial period after I left my last full-time job. I decided I was going to have fun making money in as many different ways as possible. I wrote a list of all the things I wanted to do and set about finding the work. Suddenly work had become play; an opportunity for new adventures, to meet interesting people, to get involved in a variety of interests and learn new skills.

In the past 18 months I have worked on chocolate vans at festivals, taught Spanish to Conservative MPs, been PA to one of London's top literary agents, sold burritos from a little green van in Old Street, made and sold ceramic jewellery, been flown out to Barcelona, Berlin and Athens to work at events and driven vans of all sizes all over the UK. This is no longer a trial period; I've discovered a way of earning a living that keeps me feeling alive, creative and excited every day.

And it's also given me the freedom to work on long-term projects that I wouldn't have had the time or freedom to work on if I were in a full-time job. Two years ago I got involved in a start-up social business, Careershifters, an online guide written by a group of successful career-shifters and career coaches for people wanting to change career. None of us yet get paid a wage as we turn it into a viable business, but with a portfolio career I have the flexibility to fulfil the role of content director while earning enough money to pay my bills.

Ironically, as Careershifters takes off, I may soon find myself back in the position of working five days a week and probably longer hours than ever before, but by having a portfolio career I have learned which working practices energise me and which drain me. My wellbeing is a priority these days, and through my experience of going freestyle with my career I now know exactly what I need to keep me feeling alive and excited at work.

www.careershifters.org

Toby Pellew
From property to corporate social responsibility

Like many other graduates, I had grabbed the first job offered to me, only to find it was not suitable. The trouble was I was unsure what I wanted to do, and how to go about getting it! My interests lay in politics, having studied it at university, and in sustainable development, having just returned from working on a UNESCO project in Mexico. But how to access a job which encompassed these? I had read about and understood the importance of corporate social responsibility (CSR), but trying to find a job in that field seemed almost impossible. On top of that, certain recruitment agencies were rejecting me because I had previously worked in the property sector. I felt lost and demotivated, so I contacted City Life Coaching for help.

Through a series of meetings and exercises Jenny immediately helped me focus on areas that interested me. I had become increasingly confused as to how to go about targeting the sectors that excited me, and where potential jobs could be sourced. Initially we went through my experiences, my strengths and what I ideally wanted out of my career. Essentially this meant that I was able to focus my efforts on one or two areas and sectors, whereas before my search patterns were sporadic and inefficient. Using Jenny's knowledge of my targeted sectors, we were able to produce both a long-term and a short-term objectives list, including research into certain organisations and individuals whom I would eventually go on to contact.

Jenny was great at keeping in contact and was able to answer the endless questions that I thought of after our initial meeting. We met twice more, each time giving me better clarity and understanding on where and how to look. She helped me improve my CV and, critically she was able to recommend other people to speak to about their line of work, experiences and how best to approach their sector.

It was these contacts and the direction and ongoing support/advice I got through Jenny that landed me my current role working for a corporate affairs and CSR specialist firm in London.

Brett Davidson
Advancing his own business

When I moved to the UK from Australia in 2004 I originally took a job in London with a large multinational. While the business was (and is) a fine business, and the people I worked with were great, I couldn't help feeling that my efforts were largely lost in the bigger picture. After about nine months I was really struggling there day to day because I just wasn't being fulfilled. It was then I decided to go and start my own consulting firm.

From the minute I set up things just fell into place, and nearly three years in we are further advanced as a business than I ever expected. One of the key lessons I learned was that you only need to be able to see to the horizon, not beyond it. As you walk forwards your horizon extends a little at a time, and you find your own path to success. Certainly it helps if you have a really clear vision of your desired end, but in reality I believe most small businesses evolve one small step at a time. Clarity of vision comes from doing, not constantly planning and analysing before taking any steps forward.

The only advice I have, which has been a huge part of our success to date, is to focus heavily on the marketing of your business. Your marketing efforts help you to establish a constant flow of business leads. Failure to address this early on could see you with the perfect product or service, but no one to sell it to. When the cashflow dries up the pressure mounts on small business owners, and this is when people seem to walk away saying business is not for them. By placing a strong emphasis on marketing from day one, you create momentum in that risky first two years that – by year three – gives the business a self-perpetuating life of its own.

www.fpadvance.com

Bibliography

I can personally recommend all of the books and resources below.

Part 1: Finding Your Niche

Beck, Martha, *Finding Your Own North Star: How to Claim the Life You Were Meant to Live*, Piatkus, 2001.

Berman Fortgang, Laura, *90 Days to a New Life Direction*, Piatkus, 2004.

Holden, Robert, *Success Intelligence*, Hodder & Stoughton, 2005.

Houghton, Anita, *Finding Square Holes*, Crown House Publishing, 2007.

Jansen, Julie, *I Don't Know What I Want, But I Know it's Not This*, Piatkus, 2004.

Lees, John, *How to Get a Job You'll Love*, McGraw-Hill, 2001.

Lees, John, *Take Control of your Career*, McGraw-Hill, 2006.

Moses, Barbara, *What Next?*, Dorling Kindersley, 2003.

Sher, Barbara, *I Could do Anything if only I Knew What it Was*, Dell Publishing, 1994.

Williams, Nick, *Unconditional Success: Loving the Work We Were Born to Do*, Bantam Books, 2002.

Part 2: Landing Your Perfect Job

Bolles, Richard, *What Color is Your Parachute?*, Ten Speed Press, 2007.

Chartered Management Institute, *Six Weeks to Find a Job*, Hodder & Stoughton, 2003.

Eggart, Max, *Perfect Career*, Random House, 2003.

Levy, Mike, *Presentations Made Easy*, Law Pack Publishing, 2001.

Nemko, Marty, *Cool Careers for Dummies*, Wiley Publishing, 2007.

Perkins, Graham, *Killer CVs and Hidden Approaches*, Pearson Education, 2001.

Part 3: Making an Impact

Allen, David, *Getting Things Done*, Piatkus, 2001.

Allen, David, *Ready for Anything*, Piatkus, 2003.

Buckingham, Marcus, *The One Thing You Need to Know*, Pocket Books, 2006.

Harrold, Fiona, *The 7 Rules of Success*, Hodder & Stoughton, 2006.

Kay, Frances, *Brilliant Business Connections*, How To Books, 2004.

O'Connell, Fergus, *Simply Brilliant*, Pearson Education, 2004.

O'Connell, Fergus, *How To Do a Great Job... and Go Home On Time*, Pearson Education, 2005.

Robertson, Alan, *The Fast Track Formula*, Pearson Education, 2004.

Taylor, David, *The Naked Leader Experience*, Bantam Books, 2004.

The Mind Gym, *Give Me Time*, Time Warner, 2006.

The Mind Gym, *Wake Your Mind Up*, Time Warner, 2005.

Thompson, David, *Career Helium*, Marshall Cavendish, 2007.

Part 4: Doing Your Own Thing

Barry, Amanda, *PR Power*, Virgin Books, 2002.

Dragons' Den, *Your Idea Can Make You Rich*, Vermilion, 2005.

King, Geoff, *The Secrets of Selling*, Pearson Education, 2007.

Michaels, Nancy and Karpowicz, Debbie, *Off-the-Wall Marketing Ideas*, Adams Media, 2000.

Power, Paul, *The Kitchen Table Entrepreneur*, How-To Books, 2006.

Webb, Martin, *Make Your First Million*, Capstone Publishing, 2007.

Woods, Caspian, *From Acorns: How To Build Your Brilliant Business from Scratch*, Pearson Education, 2004.

Other great books and resources

Canfield, Jack, *How To Get from Where You Are to Where You Want To Be*, HarperElement, 2007.

Cheng, Theresa, *Get Lucky! Make Your Own Opportunities*, Newleaf, 2003.

Covey, Stephen R., *The 7 Habits of Highly Effective People*, Simon & Schuster, 1989.

Ford, Bill, *High Energy Habits*, Pocket Books, 2002.

Foster, Helen, *Dejunk Your Life*, Aurum Press, 2002.

Heppell, Michael, *How To Be Brilliant*, Pearson Education, 2007.

Koch, Richard, *Living the 80/20 Way*, Nicholas Brealey Publishing, 2005.

Richardson, Cheryl, *Take Time for Your Life*, Bantam Books, 2000.

Winget, Larry, *Shut Up, Stop Whining and Get a Life*, John Wiley & Sons, 2004.

Zelinski, Ernie J., *The Lazy Person's Guide to Success*, Ten Speed Press, 2002.

www.citylifecoaching.com – the UK's leading career-coaching service for young professionals.

www.careerenergy.co.uk – another top career-coaching company, offering a wide range of services.

www.careershifters.org – helpful online resource for anyone considering a career change.

www.brightlondon.com – free career advice and support for young graduates.

www.monster.co.uk – extensive jobs database, with free CV and career advice.

www.newlifenetwork.co.uk – free advice on a wide range of career issues.

www.startups.co.uk – comprehensive advice on setting up your own business.

www.doyourownpr.com – excellent advice for anyone who wants help in promoting themselves or their business.